Finding Kluskap

Signifying (on) Scriptures, a project of the Institute for Signifying Scriptures at the Claremont Graduate University, invites and challenges scholars from different fields and disciplines to engage the phenomenon of signifying in relationship to "scriptures." The focus of these works is not upon the content meaning of texts but upon the textures, signs, material products, practices, orientations, politics, and power issues associated with the sociocultural phenomenon of the invention and engagement of scriptures. The defining interest is how peoples, especially the historically dominated, make texts signify as vectors for understanding, establishing, and communicating their identities, agency, and power in the world.

OTHER BOOKS IN THE SERIES:

Velma Love, *Divining the Self: A Study in Yoruba Myth and Human Consciousness*

Finding Kluskap

A JOURNEY INTO MI'KMAW MYTH

JENNIFER REID

THE PENNSYLVANIA STATE UNIVERSITY PRESS
UNIVERSITY PARK, PENNSYLVANIA

LIBRARY OF CONGRESS CATALOGING-IN-PUBLICATION DATA

Reid, Jennifer, 1962–
    Finding Kluskap : a journey into Mi'kmaw myth / Jennifer Reid.
        p.   cm. — (Signifying (on) Scriptures)
Summary: "Studies the mythic hero Kluskap of the Mi'kmaw people
of eastern Canada, along with a series of eighteenth-century treaties
and an annual Mi'kmaw mission to Saint Anne. Suggests that Kluskap,
the treaties, and the mission are intertwined in a way that expresses a
unique critique of modernity"—Provided by publisher.
Includes bibliographical references and index.
ISBN 978-0-271-06068-2 (cloth : alk. paper)
1. Gluskap (Legendary character).
2. Micmac mythology.
3. Micmac Indians—Government relations.
4. Micmac Indians—Social life and customs.
I. Title.

E99.M6R44 2013
398.2089'973—dc23
2013003235

The Pennsylvania State University Press is a member of the
Association of American University Presses.

It is the policy of The Pennsylvania State University Press to use
acid-free paper. Publications on uncoated stock satisfy the minimum
requirements of American National Standard for Information
Sciences—Permanence of Paper for Printed Library Material,
ANSI Z39.48–1992.

This book is printed on paper that contains 30% post-consumer waste.

For MURDENA *and* ALBERT MARSHALL

CONTENTS

ACKNOWLEDGMENTS

I wish to thank a number of people, without whom I could not have completed this book. I must express my sincere gratitude to Charles H. Long for his willingness to discuss at length the ideas that took shape around my research on Kluskap and for his insightful comments on an earlier draft of this book. His suggestions and assistance in bringing the book to publication were invaluable. I thank also Robert Choquette, as always, for the foundation he provided for me in approaching the study of Aboriginal/non-Aboriginal history in Canada. I must also gratefully acknowledge Kevin Christmas for allowing me to reprint the prophesy of the Three Crosses in this context, and Helen Sylliboy for permitting me to include her powerful poem "The Teaching of the Mi'kmaq." My thanks also to Vincent Wimbush for his critical support in getting this short and somewhat unconventional text to publication, Tatsuo Murakami for securing me copies of Japanese texts that are not available in North America, Nancy Walters and Sarah Otley for their assistance in obtaining sources that were also out of my reach, and the *Canadian Journal of Native Studies* and Brandon University for allowing me to incorporate into the first two chapters of this book material from my article "Angels of Light: A Mi'kmaq Myth in a New *Archê*," which appeared in volume 25, number 2 (2005). Finally, I must express my most profound gratitude to a number of Mi'kmaw friends, who taught me so much but who have preferred to remain anonymous in this text. And as well, and especially, I thank Murdena and Albert Marshall for the years of conversation and friendship they have given me. Every page of this book is permeated by these gifts, but they have been filtered through my own eyes, ears, and language. Therefore, I must also apologize to them and others for the inaccuracies that this text inevitably contains. These errors are mine alone.

Wela'lin.

INTRODUCTION

The Mi'kmaq of eastern Canada were the first indigenous North Americans to encounter colonial Europeans. As early as the mid-sixteenth century, they were trading with French fishers, and by the mid-seventeenth century, large numbers of Mi'kmaq had converted to Catholicism. That association would persist to varying degrees to the present day. Mi'kmaw Catholicism is exemplified by the community's regard for the figure of Saint Anne, the grandmother of Jesus.[1] Each year for a week, coinciding with the saint's feast day of July 26, Mi'kmaw peoples from communities throughout Quebec and eastern Canada gather at a small island off the coast of Nova Scotia. The island of Potlotek is the site of Canada's oldest Christian mission, and the celebration of Saint Anne on the island each July is a focal event for the community. It is, however, far from a conventional Catholic celebration. In fact, it expresses a complex set of relationships that exist between the Mi'kmaq, a cultural hero named Kluskap, a series of eighteenth-century treaties, and Saint Anne. This set of relationships is the focus of this book. In the following chapters I will relate how my desire to know something about the figure of Kluskap turned into a kind of pilgrimage. That journey ended up at Potlotek. Getting there, however, was not at all straightforward and, once I was there, the return to an original starting point was impossible.

Kluskap himself, for instance, eluded me for a long time. I came to him in the way a Western scholar often approaches an indigenous cultural form—through the lens of academic classifications. Kluskap is customarily typecast as a trickster, one of a class of mythic figures who have haunted scholarship on non-Europeans since the anthropologies of Daniel Brinton, Henry Schoolcraft, and Franz Boaz.[2] Tricksters have been described as funny characters who are lacking in conventional morality, at times benevolent and at other times unscrupulous. They are satirical figures who often mock human ways, cultural institutions, religious figures, the gods, and even themselves.[3] They are credited with creating crucial aspects of the human world, but what they create is as much a result of stupidity as it is of conscious intention. In a sense, they epitomize the highest and lowest points of human possibility: they create the world, but they also complicate it for us through their questionable behavior.[4]

In recent years tricksters have found their way into other discourses, aside from the strictly anthropological. They have, for example, been recast as embodiments of postmodernism, slippery beings who defy classical constraint. Emerging largely from nonindigenous sectors, this interpretation has relied on a kind of exoticism that has blurred the cultural contexts out of which tricksters have emerged.[5] They have also surfaced among indigenous writers and artists, cast as contemporary models for political and social action. In this work, trickster stories are no longer simply mythic tales set in the primordial past but are "parables" reflecting contemporary social contingencies and choices for action. They provide templates for resistance among indigenous peoples and, as such, are said by some to provide the trickster with a kind of ongoing animacy.[6]

Kluskap is generally classified as a trickster.[7] While it took me a while to learn anything constructive about him, one thing became clear rather quickly as I began pursuing him: if I held on to the trickster as my interpretive lens, I was going to find myself falling into a position frighteningly close to what the Métis writer Christina Fagan has characterized as fundamentally dishonest. Cultural symbols like the trickster, she writes, "can easily become labels, commodities, and stereotypes, ways of explaining and controlling that which is unfamiliar."[8]

I knew from the outset of my journey to find Kluskap that the *trickster* moniker simply was not going to hold. Although he clearly had a hand in the creation of the human world, and he had a dynamite sense of humor, he has never been unscrupulous or stupid. And I would later learn that while he can provide a model for action, this is not the primary source of his "animacy." He is, rather, a kind of mnemonic presence who not only invokes archaic structures of creation but also emerges in the modern period as a champion of Aboriginal and treaty rights. In this most important work of his, he is not so much a model as an advocate whose spirit continues to be felt.

The category of the "trickster" was an early casualty of my pilgrimage. And it was the tip of the iceberg. As with most pilgrimages, initially the goal seemed clear, but I could not predict what would transpire along the way. And once I had reached my destination, there were suddenly new issues involved in returning to where I had started. Inherent in the process were problems relating to both interpretation and epistemic boundaries, and so this book is also tacitly, but unavoidably, about a hermeneutical pilgrimage.

The question of how to interpret something requires some measure of clarity about what constitutes the subject of interpretation. In this case, one would presume that this includes Kluskap, Saint Anne, and the treaties. But herein lies a bit of complexity. In chapter 4, I will raise the issue of a reflection on religion and modernity that appears to be embedded in the Saint Anne's Day Mission—a critique that is enmeshed in the treaties that are both artifacts of the eighteenth-century colonial landscape of Atlantic Canada and blueprints for present and future postcolonial relationships in the Canadian state. While Kluskap, Saint Anne, and the treaties immediately pertain to the Mi'kmaw community, from my vantage point as a non-Native scholar they appear to be also unavoidably implicated in this evaluation of the broader society in which the community finds itself. Moreover, it seems to me that this critique presents a direct challenge to many of the discourses about religion and modernity that hold sway among contemporary academics. But this raises a question: what is at stake in my reflection on these broader cultural and academic implications and my writing about them? I can say with relative certainty that they are not central concerns among Mi'kmaw peoples. Five hundred years of colonial contact has not instilled in this community a driving need to have non-Mi'kmaw peoples "get it." At the same time, my Mi'kmaw friends were willing to share some part of "it" with me, hoping, I suppose, that I would proceed to use that knowledge to better understand our shared situation as modern peoples. So where has that left me in terms of the subject of interpretation? Essentially, I have found myself left with a distinct sense that regardless of how much I can know about Mi'kmaw culture, this book is also unavoidably self-referential. As Charles H. Long puts it, "Every adequate hermeneutic is at heart an essay in self-understanding. It is the effort to understand the self through the mediation of the other."[9]

Of course, the issue I am raising is nothing new. The conventional way of dealing with it among academics has been to stake out fixed positionalities:

etic/emic, insider/outsider. But in this case, these simply do not work. To be sure, I am an outsider. I am writing as an academic, and a good deal of the research underpinning this book involves anthropological and historical sources written from the seventeenth century onward. More critically, the scholarly tradition I represent is implicated in a centuries-long process of marginalization of indigenous cultures—the so-called primitives that lie at the ideological foundation of the rise of the West and, no less, of the modern study of religion and other disciplines in the humanities. I am rooted in both a cultural history and an academic culture that approached indigenous peoples in the modern period as either extraneous to the emergence of the West (hence the marginalization of indigenous peoples generally) or as raw material for cultural expansion (for example, the slave trade and the academic disciplines). In recent decades, Mi'kmaw peoples have generally abandoned an earlier willingness to engage the questions and research of non-Native scholars. They have simply tired of talking with people who went on to write books and articles that they never saw. Academics took what they heard from Native "informants" and then filled in the blanks to create narratives and descriptions that appealed to the tastes and sensitivities of non-Native readers. Additionally, academics too rarely raised issues or expressed frames of mind that pointed to the reciprocal character of both their relationship with their subjects and the "data" they had collected. An important point here is that there were indeed blanks.

Modern scholars and indigenous peoples came together in the first instance because European colonials had engaged in a permanent occupation of the non-European world. Indigenous spaces became contact zones and transcultural spaces. Mary Louise Pratt has described these as arenas in which "people geographically and historically separated come into contact with one another and establish on-going relations, usually involving conditions of coercion, radical inequality, and intractable conflict."[10] In Canada, this conquest also entailed a presumption on the part of dominant sectors of the society that First Nations peoples could be geographically situated, culturally remade, and legally defined. Reserves (radically reduced tracts allotted to First Nations from their original heritage of land) ensured that Native peoples would be removed from the areas occupied by non-Natives. The Canadian government's Indian Act of 1876 legislatively objectified First Nations peoples through the assumption of government control over virtually every aspect of life on reserves. The government prohibited dancing and other religious activity, for example; it specified who was and who was not an "Indian"; and it designated how bands could be governed and how land could be disposed of. While it has undergone amendment, the Indian Act remains a vehicle for exercising these forms of control. A residential school system, jointly administered by the federal government and the churches, and in place until the second half of the twentieth century, subjected generations of Aboriginal children to degradation and abuse, stripping them of their languages, tribal knowledge, and family relationships. In short, First Nations peoples have contended with a dominant culture that has consistently assumed that "Indians" could be defined and remade into integers consistent with colonial and postcolonial policies. These acts of definition are not, however, knowledge. The lack of cultural reciprocity (legal, social, and scholarly) that has characterized Native and non-Native relationships has ensured that critical aspects of collective Native self-knowledge have, for the sake of cultural survival, remained concealed and protected within their communities.

Time and again, as I looked for Kluskap, I was told that there were things I simply could not know. Cultural knowledge is not a product; it is the surplus that comes of reciprocal relationships. So, while I have stories to relate and events to describe in this book that have not found their way into other scholarly literature, I also embody the history of the West and because of this, there are limits to what I can—and should—know. Am I then an "outsider?" Do I have an "etic" point of view? Not entirely. I have a story to relate and a hermeneutical claim to stake here that are surpluses of a particular set of relationships I have with friends who are Mi'kmaq. But I do not pretend that these reflect a comprehensive understanding of a complex cultural expression or that they are even the sum total of our respective positionalities. They are, simply, surpluses accruing from the reciprocal nature of our relationship. As such, they point to a kind of understanding or knowledge gleaned from within what the historian of religions Joachim Wach would have described as "an intermediate field between the entirely foreign and the perfectly familiar."[11] The stories I learned, the memories of the past that were recalled in my presence, the sacred moments in which I was permitted to share were all offered in friendship. My questions that went unanswered, however, remained so because of a historical legacy of which I am unshakably a part. In other words, the contact zone out of which this book arises defies conventional classification with respect to scholarly perspective.

In writing this book, I have had to think a great deal about transcultural spaces. I have begun to think of such spaces as generally "metamorphic," acknowledging my debt here to Davíd Carrasco, who has employed the term in relation to visions of place (which I will consider more fully later).[12] A metamorphosis is a kind of second birth through which an organism undergoes an obvious and sudden transformation. In most cases, that organism can no longer fully function in its old environment; one example is the salmon, which must seek out salt—rather than fresh—water. What I find most helpful in thinking about transcultural spaces as metamorphic is that the analogy directs our attention to the radical nature of the contact zone, its relationship to things that came before, its re-creation of the human environment, and its role in the generation of profoundly new modes of being a human. Of course, anyone who has ever stopped long enough to watch, say, a butterfly emerge from a chrysalis, also knows that the operation is not entirely pretty. In fact, it is a conflicted, almost painful process to witness.

We know that the European incursion into the Americas created that kind of painful rupture and new beginning. At the same time, it created a new hermeneutical situation, one that Charles Long describes as "a situation in which *Homo Americanus* was continually trying to discover and decipher the meaning of existence in the context of the most intense new and radical experience of Western humanity."[13] In many respects the Saint Anne's Day Mission, which was the terminus of sorts in my search for Kluskap, confronts this kind of New World dilemma. But this book is equally a product of a hermeneutical situation. The space and time out of which it emerged was itself a transcultural and metamorphic context. Stories were shared, and others were withheld. New questions were generated, and others were abandoned. At times there was camaraderie and reciprocity, and at other times reticence, misgivings, and distrust. As a result, this book does not present a total portrait of a community's sacred life, nor does it provide a comprehensive and novel hermeneutic. My guess is that it is fragmentary at best on both counts. The fact is, I don't really know. And perhaps that's just as it should be.

1

TREATIES AND AQUATIC PARASITES

In 2002 I was asked to take part in a panel discussion at the annual meeting of the American Academy of Religion. The panel was to be a recognition of the fortieth anniversary of the publication of Charles H. Long's *Alpha: The Myths of Creation*, a book that has been published in numerous editions and has become a standard work among historians of religion.[1] In thinking about my presentation, I decided that I would turn to *Alpha* as an entrée into a discussion of Kluskap, a mythic hero among the Mi'kmaq of northeastern North America. In spite of a flurry of ethnographic work focused on Kluskap in the nineteenth and early to mid-twentieth centuries, he has not received much scholarly attention in recent years. So I decided that I would consider current Kluskap myths in light of *Alpha*. It seemed to me that the plan was relatively straightforward, but I could not have been more mistaken. The research I began at that time led me on a journey that would last for a number of years and ultimately leave me somewhere far removed from where I would have imagined in 2002. In retrospect this seems somehow appropriate, given that *Alpha* is a book in which journeys of all kinds figure prominently. There are human journeys from formless potential, through various nonhuman places and modes, to fully human existences in a human worlds.[2] There are journeys of divine beings from places of primordial chaos to the order of the natural world and journeys from water, darkness, or embryonic modes to earth, light, or *being* of some form or another.[3] My own journey now seems appropriate, too, since I was pursuing Kluskap—a figure who, whatever else may be said of him, was continually on the move.

Envisioning my American Academy of Religion presentation, I imagined an exercise in which I would wed certain aspects of *Alpha* with the figure of Kluskap. And I was initially fairly confident that this would be an uncomplicated project. From written accounts of nineteenth- and early twentieth-century missionaries, journalists, travelers, and ethnographers, I had learned that this ancient hero of the Mi'kmaq had given animals and birds their voices, he had created the wind that moved the water, and he had made great rocks and chasms simply by blowing smoke from his pipe.[4] According to some accounts, Kluskap was one of a set of primordial twins who had to outwit and murder his evil brother to avoid being killed by him.[5] Among his most spectacular exploits was his journey up a great river with his lifelong companions, Marten and Grandmother Bear. The cliffs suddenly began to close around them, and the water began to flow downward into the earth, the river becoming increasingly narrow and tempestuous, the deadly current pulling the three voyagers down through rocks and ravines. Marten and Grandmother died from fear, but Kluskap continued to guide the canoe through the night until he broke into sunlight. When he reached the shore, he carried his companions to a wigwam, where he brought them back to life.[6] Prior to his leaving the Mi'kmaq, it was said that he rid the world of primordial monsters, cleared rivers for navigation, and taught the people all they needed to know to survive in their world.[7]

In the summer of 2002, with a presentation hanging over me, Kluskap seemed almost too good to be true. He was one of a set of primordial twins representing good and evil; he had descended into watery chaos to bring regeneration; he had taught human beings to know themselves. Resonating with the scenario of primal hostility between divine figures that Long had presented in *Alpha,* here was a situation in which "an evil brother seems to posses greater physical power, [but] he cannot finally defeat the good twin"; and, again, reverberating with Long's discussion of mythic descent into water, Kluskap's journey down the great river was "analogous to a descent into the underworld or a return to the womb. The purpose of such descents into the unformed and chaotic is renewal and stability." In addition, a story concerning Kluskap's birth (which I will consider more fully later) mirrored precisely those myths that Long described in which the "evil twin refuses to be born in the usual manner and breaks through the side of the mother, killing her."[8] It thus seemed merely incumbent upon me to find current Kluskap stories to be able to speak a little about the way in which this hero—and, by extension, a traditional mythic framework—had kept up with the times. This research, I thought, could serve a couple of purposes. The most immediate of course was to provide me with something constructive to say at the American Academy of Religion meeting with respect to a book that warranted serious recognition. In so doing, however, I hoped not only to speak to that occasion but also to consider a figure that to my mind had been the recipient of a good deal of misrepresentation within a relatively meager scholarly literature: the hero Kluskap.

This is not to say that he has been wholly absent from publishers' catalogs in recent years. To be sure, a number of Kluskap stories have appeared in collections over the past few decades. Alden Nowlan, for example, recorded a Kluskap story in his *Nine Micmac Legends* (1983), a collection of stories based on Silas Rand's nineteenth-century accounts; and Ruth Holmes Whitehead included a number of myths dating to the 1890s and 1930s in her *Stories from the Six Worlds* (1988). The historian Daniel Paul referred to early twentieth-century stories in his *We Were Not the Savages* (1993); and Rita Joe and Leslie Choyce included a story from Whitehead's collection, as well as one story as told by the poet Mary-Louise Martin, in their *Mi'kmaq Anthology* (1997). Rita Joe (poet laureate of the Mi'kmaq, who received the Order of Canada in 1990) also wrote of Kluskap in her collection *Song of Eskasoni*; and Michael Runningwolf and Patricia Clark Smith in 2000 published *On the Trail of Elder Brother,* an entire collection of Kluskap myths based on stories Runningwolf heard as a child.[9]

While stories about Kluskap continue to appear in published form (though much of this draws on myths that were first published a century or more ago), very few scholars have chosen to write about him, and among those who have (principally since 2002), the work has not been particularly comprehensive. The largest body of scholarship on Kluskap has been written by Anne-Christine Hornborg, a scholar with an abiding interest in a public demonstration mounted by a group of Mi'kmaw warriors in 1990. This event spurred her to produce a substantial body of work dealing with issues relating to Mi'kmaw identity and the mythic hero.[10] The 1990 demonstration involved a Mi'kmaw warrior society led by Sulian Stone Eagle Herney that attempted to subvert a proposed plan to create a rock quarry on Cape Breton Island, Nova Scotia. The plan was the brainchild of Kelly Rock, a company that intended to create a "superquarry" on Kelly's Mountain, a site that is sacred to Mi'kmaw people because of its association with Kluskap. The warrior society first demonstrated against the company in 1989. When it appeared that Kelly Rock was not to be dissuaded, the men mounted another demonstration in 1990, this time dressed in military fatigues and announcing that they were "preparing for war."[11] This demonstration was undoubtedly a contributing factor in Kelly Rock's decision to scrap the plan for a superquarry, and the media attention that Herney and the other warriors received at that time was undeniably warranted.

Hornborg, however, has made too much of the 1990 event with respect to Kluskap, having published extensively on the subject for a number of years (while often steering conspicuously away from the salient issue of religion). Her article "Readbacks or Tradition," for instance, is a study of the relationship between contemporary understandings of Kluskap and non-Native accounts of the hero and, more specifically, the extent to which "readback" figures in Mi'kmaw accounts.[12] A series of interviews with persons who were involved in the Kelly's Mountain demonstration in 1990 provided the bulk of her primary research material for this essay; in fact, she did not explore any contemporary meanings of Kluskap aside from his association with the mountain and the protest. This was clearly a miscalculation, since the warrior society did not represent the entire Mi'kmaw community. A 1994 episode of the Canadian Broadcasting Corporation's television program *The Fifth Estate,* for instance, was focused on Stone Eagle Herney, and it highlighted this lack of consensus. Mi'kmaw elder Murdena Marshall, introduced to the television audience as "a Harvard-educated specialist in Native studies," said this rather explicitly. "I think he [Stone Eagle Herney] wants to be seen . . . as a person that knows the culture inside out. That he's an expert on Micmac's values, tradition, and language." Asked how much truth there was in that attitude, Professor Marshall answered, "Not much. . . . There's a lot of potential for Hollywood."[13]

Hornborg's argument, based on a rather circumscribed body of evidence, is that Kluskap is a part of Mi'kmaw tradition rather than a religious figure.[14] This conclusion is simply unjustifiable. It is, nonetheless, an assumption that permeates her work, finding full expression in her 2008 book *Mi'kmaq Landscapes,* in which she pits tradition and modernity against one another, claiming that "traditionalists" (typified by the warrior society) are redefining Mi'kmaw culture.[15] Traditionalists also figure in her work on the Saint Anne's Day Mission (an important celebration that I will consider later in this book), along with Kluskap. Again, there are problems with this work. Hornborg claims that Kluskap stories were being told in the seventeenth century and thus contributed to the propagation of Catholicism among the Mi'kmaq. But there is no documentary evidence to support this claim, and she cites no oral history that might mitigate this unavoidable issue.[16]

Like Anne-Christine Hornborg, Alf Hornborg has been uneasy with the religious implications of Kluskap. In an article on the superquarry plan, Alf Hornborg directed his attention to a subject that would, ultimately, become a concern underlying my own research, and represented in this book: the relationship between modernity, identity, discourse, and power. Our conclusions, however, are dramatically different, principally because Hornborg assumes a kind of reductionism that undercuts the authenticity of religious life—something that I am not prepared to do. He argues that religion is a mechanism deployed in the service of social resistance, and he thus regards it as an abstract idea that is "radically opposed to modernity, and commoditization because it posits irreplaceable and incommensurable values."[17] Although I am tempted at this point to raise the issue of whose modernity Hornborg is speaking about, I will save that discussion for a later chapter.

Aside from this work, research on Kluskap has been scant. The most unusual work has undoubtedly been done by two Japanese scholars, Yoichi Higashikawa and Masatsugu Kimura, whose articles have not been available in North America.[18] In the early 1990s, the two scholars published a couple of articles that included a transcription of a Kluskap myth told by Steven Augustine at a powwow in New Brunswick in 1992, as well as a commentary on the story in which they attempted to compare it with other Kluskap myths "in detail." The work was unremarkable in this respect, as they consulted only two sources for stories (one of which sources contained only one story); but its creative incorporation of Augustine's story (which they regarded as "moralistic" rather than "mythical") into their own interpretive frameworks marked by "spiritualism" and "Ghost Worlds" was an interesting exercise in Japanese-Mi'kmaq cultural metamorphosis (a broader subject that I will be considering in greater detail in the final chapter of this book).

In 2002, it seemed to me that a study of Kluskap was not unjustified. I had no grand plan for this research, however. I simply wanted to hear some stories and reflect on them a little. The plan, as I mentioned already, was pretty naive. During the summer preceding the meeting, I set about asking a number of friends for stories; and although everyone I approached agreed to help me out, our conversations never quite found their way to Kluskap. In fact, I never managed to hear a single Kluskap story. It began to dawn on me that I had heard a substantial number of Mi'kmaw stories over the past decade and could recall only a couple of occasions when Kluskap figured in these. When I asked about this, friends confirmed what I was beginning to suspect: that the stories were not necessarily at the forefront of their thoughts. I had begun the project with the assumption that Kluskap was a central figure in Mi'kmaw discourse, but as conversations transpired it became apparent that my assumption was based substantially on published documents dating from the mid-nineteenth to the mid-twentieth centuries, rather than on anything I had actually heard.

A few years earlier, in his book *Weaving Ourselves into the Land* Tom Parkhill had explored the nineteenth-century Kluskap myths recorded by Charles Leland and their impact on the study of myth. At this juncture, it seemed to me more than ever before that he was onto something critical. Leland's tales, Parkhill argued, were formative for subsequent folklorists, appearing in abridged or adapted forms in early works such as Lewis Spence's *The Myths of the North American Indians* (1914) and later ones like Joseph Campbell's *Historical Atlas of World Mythology* (1988).[19] Campbell's version undoubtedly reached the widest audience, but Spence's text was also reprinted into the 1990s in Canada, the United States, and Britain. In considering Leland's influence, Parkhill suggested that the Kluskap tales appealed to non-Native readers because of their dualistic (European) structure, as well as their capacity to speak to conquest and place needs of colonial peoples. Parkhill had identified a critical problem for those of us now reading these myths, namely, that the interpretive lenses of these writers were almost certainly not those of their "informants." As Ruth Holmes Whitehead has pointed out, language was also unmistakably an issue too. Very few existing versions of the stories were recorded by Mi'kmaw people, and most of those who recorded them had no knowledge of the Mi'kmaw language.[20]

The problem of interpretation is fairly obvious when it comes to Kluskap, and Leland is as good a place to start as any in terms of addressing the issue. For Leland, the hero was the "lord Glooscap," an object of Mi'kmaw worship who was also the "grandest and most Aryan character ever evolved from a savage mind," a figure who could easily be grasped by anyone familiar with Beowulf or the work of Shakespeare and Rabelais.[21] Leland was not the only writer of the period to take this kind of license with Kluskap. Virtually all those who recorded these stories stressed the divinity of this "most illustrious of the deities of the Micmacs, after the Great Spirit . . . a demigod, who exercised omnipotence."[22] More problematically, they also stressed the relationship of his stories with those of other cultural traditions, in some cases even causally. Reflecting on his initial attempts to collect Algonkian legends, for instance, Leland later wrote that he had not expected to find much. He was consequently surprised to discover a body of oral literature that was, he claimed, ancient and much "grander" than that of any other North American tribe. He believed that the stories he collected bore a distinct resemblance to Scandinavian folktales, a phenomenon he attributed to direct historical transmission. He consequently concluded that Kluskap was a "demigod" who had more in common with Odin and Thor than with other North American mythic figures and that he was "the Norse god intensified."[23]

For William Elder and M. F. Sweetser, who recorded stories a decade earlier than Leland, Kluskap was "an Indian Prometheus" and a "new Arion"; and for Stansbury Hagar, who wrote at the turn of the twentieth century, Kluskap was an example of the universal "solar hero" who emerges from a cave at night and disappears into the West at daylight, only to return again. Hagar added that he was also a member of a trinity of heroes who were actually a single sky god "named in three differing aspects." Hagar's contemporary Luther Roth believed that in certain Kluskap legends, he could hear echoes of biblical stories, and he concluded that they may well have been "derived from that source."[24] And as late as 1969, the historian Alfred Goldsworthy Bailey claimed that at certain times Kluskap was "confused with Noah. . . . There is a period of the Law before the coming of Christ in which he had to be obeyed, and it is generally as an Old Testament figure that he appears in the adulterated tales. . . . In the tale of Gluskap's journey Hebrew and Micmac elements are well mingled."[25]

Whatever else we might say about the Kluskap who emerged from this literature (and I will say more presently), we can safely conclude that those who recorded the stories went to considerable lengths to connect the hero with those of other European literatures with which they were familiar. The question of why they did this obviously cannot be unequivocally answered, but I would suggest a couple of related possibilities: first, the basic need to find a common symbolic language and, second, the desire to impose a linear form on what was a digressive body of stories in order to mitigate the possibility that the writers had very little idea of what was actually going on. What they could not have helped but notice was that there was no coherent Kluskap narrative in which to situate the myths they heard. There is no avoiding the fact that one of the most obvious links between the stories they heard was that they were continually changing. Certain characters or motifs became nuclei from which other stories unfolded or to which other stories attached themselves. Some myths seemed to absorb others, characters gained prominence and then lost it, and European cultural elements (monarchs, warships, etc.) figured increasingly as time went on.[26] Only one early folklorist, Elsie Clews Parsons, seems to have been fully at ease with this fact. Referring to stories she had collected at the turn of the twentieth century, she wrote, "A number of incidents were related about Gluskap . . . but no continuous narrative. In fact I doubt if sequence or adventure or continuity is associated with Gluskap in the minds of most people. They refer now to one anecdote, now to another; and one anecdote may suggest another, but the anecdotes do not thread or piece together as in a regular tale."[27]

Parsons's observation was particularly appropriate with respect to those stories that dealt with the birth of Kluskap, as well as those that spoke of his departure from Mi'kmakik (the land of the Mi'kmaq). In 1864 a travel writer and sportsman, Arthur Gordon, published a narrative of a hunting expedition called "Wilderness Journeys in New Brunswick," in which he included a number of Kluskap stories that had been told to him by his Native guides. Gordon's article contained the earliest recorded story of Kluskap's birth, and it offered little by way of explanation. "Long time ago, in the ages which are passed away, lived the great twin brethren, Clote Scarp [Kluskap] and Mulsunsis. That was in the days of the great beaver, feared by beasts and men; and in that time there was but one language among all things living. Now whence came the brethren, or what their origin, no man nor beast knew, nor ever shall know;—nay, they knew it not themselves."

Gordon went on to record at length the story of a primordial deception that occurred between the brothers. "But it came to pass, that as Mulsunsis thought of these things day by day, it came into his mind to slay his brother, that he alone might be great among beasts and men; and envy of his brother began to eat up his heart." Ultimately, Malsum makes three failed attempts on his brother's life before Kluskap is forced to kill him to save himself. "Then Clote Scarp rose up and took a fern-root in his hand, and sought out his brother, and said: 'Why dost thou thus seek my life? So long as thou knewest not I had not fear, but now thou must die, for thou hast learned my secret, and I cannot trust thee.' And he smote him with the fern root, and Mulsunsis fell down dead. And Clote Scarp sang a song over him and lamented."[28]

The missionary Silas Rand, whose collection of Mi'kmaq myths and legends was the most comprehensive of the nineteenth century, recorded a similar story (to which I referred briefly at the outset of the chapter). In this version, however, the twins were well aware of where they had come from. "Glooscap was one of twins. Before they were born, they conversed and consulted together how they would better enter the world. Glooscap determined to be born naturally; the other resolved to burst through his mother's side. These plans were carried into effect. Glooscap was first born; the mother died, killed by the younger as he burst the walls of his prison. The two boys grew up together, miraculously preserved."[29]

Working from a nine-hundred-page folio of Mi'kmaw stories lent to him by Rand, Leland recounted much the same story that would later appear in Rand's collection, with a few differences. The most notable in this respect was his claim that "the first birth was of Glooskap, the Good principle, and Malsum the Wolf, or Evil principle. The Wolf was born from his mother's armpit. He is sometimes male and sometimes female."[30] Michael Runningwolf, in his collection of Kluskap stories recalled from his childhood, included a similar story that emphasized Kluskap's identification with humanity:

> Before they came into this world, the two babies held council with one another in their mother's womb. They talked about the different ways they wanted to be born. Glous'gap said "I choose to be born in the usual way, just as other babies are." He knew that it would be his job to lead the people, and being born in the way of an ordinary child would help him to be closer to them.
>
> But Young Wolf thought himself too great a being to come forth into the world in such a common manner. He vowed "When my time arrives, I shall burst out through our mother's armpit."[31]

An entirely different explanation for Kluskap's birth appeared in Frank Speck's 1915 article in the *Journal of American Folk-Lore*, a story based on narratives provided by two men, Joe Julian and John Joe. "Gluskap was the god of the Micmacs. The great deity, Ktcini'sxam, made him out of earth and then breathed on him, and he was made. This was at Cape North (Kte'dnuk, 'At the North Mountain'), Cape Breton, on the eastern side."[32] Another version appeared in Parsons's article in the same journal a decade later (though she had heard the story twenty-five years earlier). "The time that Christ made the world, it was dark, so he made the stars. It was not bright enough then, so he made the moon. Brighter, but not like day, he made the sun then. He put his own shadow on to the water of the bay, so it would rise into the sky to be the sun. . . . [Then] he took the earth and made a man [Kluskap]."[33]

Yet another version was recorded in the mid-1920s by Clara Dennis, a journalist who worked for the Halifax *Herald*. Dennis's work is of particular note because, of all the ethnographic material we have from this period, hers is thought to be perhaps the least affected by her own interpretative lenses. Between 1923 and 1929, Dennis conducted a series of interviews with a Mi'kmaw medicine man by the name of Jerry Lonecloud. In the context of these interviews, Lonecloud (who was also, from 1910 until 1940, the principle Mi'kmaw advisor to the Provincial Museum of Nova Scotia) shared his knowledge of Mi'kmaw language, medicine, folklore, and myths, and Dennis recorded this information in a number of field notebooks she kept during the period.[34] It is fairly safe to assume that these notebooks contain a great deal of material that can be traced directly to Lonecloud. However, we should note that Dennis had no apparent problem with manipulating this material to serve her own writing agendas. In 1942, for instance, she published an account of a trip to Chapel Island, Nova Scotia, at the time of the annual Saint Anne's Day Mission, during which she spoke with a chief who showed her a pipe and copies of some treaties. After explaining to her that the pipe was smoked in the context of the meeting of the Sante' Wawio'mi (the Grand Council) to commemorate peace with the Mohawk, he went on to discuss the treaties that represented peace with the British. "The chief showed me, too, the old parchment treaty. 'We get it from King long ago to keep it and honour it and serve it and follow it,' the old chief said." A discussion between Dennis and the chief may well have occurred at the time of the mission, but his statement regarding the treaty most certainly did not. That part of the narrative was borrowed from a story told to her by Jerry Lonecloud a decade or more earlier, a story that she had recorded in one of her field books at that time.[35] That said, I believe that we can read these notebooks themselves in relative confidence that they represent Lonecloud's words. In fact, her use of them in the 1942 text (despite the attribution to a "chief") simply indicates that his story was better than any Dennis heard when she later attended the mission herself.

Lonecloud's explanation for Kluskap's birth stressed the fact that Kluskap was the first human being, albeit an undeniably special one, and the myths he shared with Dennis highlight particularly well the lack of narrative coherence when it comes to this figure.[36] On one occasion, for instance, he told the journalist:

Here's about the origin of man. How we come here.

Kji-kinap was first He made everything, and then he took a rest and lay on the ground to see what he had done. He found a stone image like a person, and it looked so perfect. . . . He come up to it, and it looked so like a man he spoke to it and asked "What are you doing here?" No response. Asked the second time and no response. Third time he stooped and blew his breath in the image's mouth. The image came to.

Adam made out of mud, not so good. Stone is better. . . .

. . . The stone came alive like a person. Kji-kinap said, "Sit up, stand up!" and the image walked. Then he said, "I'm going to name you. Your name is Kluskap.[37]

Some time later, however, Lonecloud told the following story: "Bishops and others have various theories as to our origin. They say we came from places like China or the Bering Strait. But we know where we come from—the sky. The young man answered, 'I come from the sky.' . . . *Our* forefathers come from the sky. Adam and Eve come from the earth. So the Indians all come from the sky, and we always believed that we come this way into civilization, as you call it."[38] Runningwolf would recall something similar with respect to Kluskap's appearance in our world. "Some say that Glous'gap was born in the land of the Wabenaki, but more ancient stories speak of him coming down from Was'ouk, the Sky World, during the time the world was being formed by Kesoulk, the Creator."[39]

Like the myths of Kluskap's creation, those concerning his departure are extremely varied. Rand, for instance, wrote that he had gone away but that the people knew neither why nor where he had actually gone.[40] According to Gordon, however, he left because "the ways of beasts and men waxed evil, and they greatly vexed Clote Scarp, and at length he could no longer endure them. And he made a great feast by the shore of the great lake—all the beasts came to it—and when the feast was over he got into a big canoe, he and his uncle, the great turtle, and they went away over the big lake, and the beasts looked after them until they saw them no more."[41]

Leland's version of the myth was borrowed almost verbatim from Gordon, although a couple of variations are worth noting: Leland identified the big lake as "the great lake Minas," and he wrote that Kluskap had left on his own.[42] A version that appeared in a contemporary travel guide was the first to identify Kluskap's broad dissatisfaction with a particular group of people: the hero left on his own, according to the guide, because of "the approach of the English."[43] Roth's 1891 account was more specific with respect to his motive: "But the mighty Glooscap was not able to cope with the white invaders who came into his domain. He was vexed with the English beyond all endurance. And the end of the matter was that once, in a mighty storm, he broke down his beaver dam, kicked over his camp-kettle, which is now known as Spencer's Island, turned his two huge dogs into stone, left them standing on the mountains, and took an unceremonious departure."[44]

Some versions simply said that Kluskap disappeared into the west when he had finished teaching the Mi'kmaq.[45] But others linked his departure with prophecies concerning the future arrival of Europeans. According to Speck, for example, Kluskap told the Mi'kmaq, "I am going to leave you. I am going to a place where I can never be reached by a white man. Then he prophesied the coming of the Europeans and the baptism of the Micmacs." Speck was also clear about where Kluskap went: "Then he called his grandmother, from Pictou, and a young man for his nephew, and departed, going to the other side of the North Pole with them. . . . When Peary discovered the North Pole, he saw Gluskap sitting at the top of the Pole, and spoke to him."[46]

Again, for both Lonecloud and Runningwolf, prophesy figured notably in Kluskap's withdrawal. According to Lonecloud, "Glooscap said there will be white people come and take your land from you but I go to make you a happy hunting ground and there shall be no other nation enter it then there shall be no one to molest you."[47] In this account, Kluskap traveled alone after turning his grandmother to stone at Cape Split.[48] Runningwolf's was equally tragic: "In enormous canoes bearded men are coming across the Great Waters of the Sunrise. Those wooden canoes are as many as the snowflakes of winter. These people are white, and they are like hungry, unenlightened children. They will take this land and its lakes and forests away from you. They will almost destroy it."[49]

I have presented these two examples concerning Kluskap's birth and his departure to underscore the point that, given the array of often contradictory elements that characterized Kluskap myths that were recorded during the period, it is not unreasonable to suggest that many of those who recorded them were at a bit of a loss about how to coherently relate them to one another. In many of these cases, the link between the stories was an imported frame of reference pointing to ancient European mythologies or British and continental literatures. As I began my *Alpha* project I quickly became uneasy with these Kluskap texts and increasingly convinced of the necessity of hearing contemporary stories against which I might be able to measure the earlier ones. What I would not figure out until some time later is that all these myths shared some fundamental resonances in spite of both their variations and the interpretive vantage points of those who recorded them. There is indeed something noticeably coherent about Kluskap myths, but it does not hinge on chronology or consistency of obvious narrative content. What I would discover is that while a community's self-understanding might well be articulated within the structures of any particular body of myth, the relationship between individual myths is no more predictable than the experience of the world in which that community finds itself. This realization, however, took some time. Meanwhile, I focused my attention on looking for stories. And, as I said, from the moment I started I was vaguely aware that I was on a journey to somewhere different from where I had anticipated.

I initially approached friends at Eskasoni, Nova Scotia, hoping to hear a Kluskap story. Instead, I was told about a variety of other things. I heard, for instance, about a new academic program at the University College of Cape Breton called Toqwa'tu'kl Kjijitaqnn (Integrated Science), which had been designed to blend conventional methods and data from the natural sciences (biology, geology, chemistry, physics, and cosmology) with the knowledge system of the Mi'kmaq.[50] Since some elders of the community were involved with this degree program from its inception, I was encouraged to speak with them regarding the goals and content of the program; and I did so, secretly harboring hope still that I might be able to hear a Kluskap story. From Murdena Marshall, I discovered that the program had emerged from an idea for a single course in 1991. The course was offered for the first time in 1995, and in the spring of 2002 the university had graduated its first Bachelor of Science students with a concentration in Integrated Science. When I asked about the content of the course, Murdena reflected on the fact that the Milky Way can be defined by Western science from a number of perspectives, but it is never explained by conventional science in terms of its purpose. The Milky Way, she pointed out, changes its angle in the spring and fall from diagonal to vertical, and it does this to guide the Canada geese in their migrations. As a rule, she said, Western sciences do not ask *why* when approaching the natural world; or, to put it another way, these sciences do not traditionally account for the significance of natural phenomena with respect to the world that human beings meaningfully inhabit.[51]

Since Murdena's husband, Albert Marshall, had been instrumental in constructing the first course syllabus for an Integrated Science course, I proceeded to ask him about the content of the program. Albert replied that

Mi'kmaw children are no longer able to learn their tribal knowledge in the way that previous generations had. Their lives are characterized by a kind of perpetual motion, and they are inundated with video games and a drive toward consumerism. Sitting for hours at an elder's table for the purpose of education is no longer a viable option for many children.[52] Others would later add that even if children were inclined toward this form of education, illness (especially diabetes) has become so acute in the community of Eskasoni that the number of elders is decreasing noticeably. The average life expectancy at Eskasoni is less than forty years, with more than half of the community's population under thirty years old. Albert went on to say that the scientific community alone has real efficacy in influencing public and private sector policy toward the environment and that it is imperative that Native people enter into this community in order to arrest the destruction of the natural world that is being enacted under the aegis of capital gain. Waving toward a window looking out on a bay, Albert said, "The oysters are sick."

The oysters were indeed sick in the Brasdor Lakes, a group of salt-water lakes in Cape Breton Island, on one of which Eskasoni First Nation is located. Cape Breton oysters were hit with MSX disease in the fall of 2002, and stocks were subsequently devastated. The disease was dumped into Little Narrows at that time, along with ballast water from Chesapeake Bay ships that was riddled with the parasite; and it was then spreading to Prince Edward Island, threatening one of the province's most essential industries.[53] The disease was identified in Delaware in the late 1950s and along with another disease, Dermo, has often caused a 50 percent annual mortality rate. Funding for research has been inadequate, and in fifty years researchers have succeeded only in developing population and disease models and identifying certain triggers.[54] They have not identified the parasite's infective stage, its lifestyle, or other critical factors relating to time, water temperature, and levels of salinity. They have also been unable to engage in controlled transmission of the parasite, and they have concerns that an unidentified intermediate host may exist. In practical terms, scientists have been able to suggest only that disease-resistant oyster strains should be farmed and that these should be maintained in disease-free areas.[55] This is not much to show for a half century of research, but at the very least it should have been sufficient to compel governing bodies to pay attention to environmental agencies that have been calling for controls on ballast water. Although some United States coastal regions had stopped Chesapeake Bay ships from discharging their ballast, the Canadian government had chosen not to follow this route, and the oysters at Eskasoni—a community whose economy relies heavily on aquaculture—were dying. Albert believed that the oysters were emblematic: much of the world is being destroyed in a similar fashion, and the destruction rests on the Western premise that non-human entities are objects. He was convinced that the scientific community and its financial resources could be made to work for the Mi'kmaq and for the environment by introducing—and demonstrating the viability of—the Mi'kmaw understanding of nonhuman entities as subjects. The sustainability of any species was critical, from Albert's vantage point, because of the integration of all species. Besides, he added, it also made long-term economic sense.

Our discussion of the content and goals of Toqwa'tu'kl Kjijitaqnn involved the Milky Way, elders, and MSX disease, in the context of which another attempt to mention Kluskap went by the wayside. Not to be dissuaded, I approached friends yet again with questions about Kluskap. I wanted to know, primarily, if anyone speaks of him in ways that resemble the stories recorded by the writers of the nineteenth and early twentieth centuries. A number of people told me that Kluskap is a figure associated primarily with landscape. Others, however, for reasons I could not quite fathom, spoke about Saint Anne, the grandmother of Jesus and the patron saint of the Mi'kmaw people. It was a segue that caught me off guard, not least because of the reverence with which they spoke. While many among the present generation of Mi'kmaq were baptized Roman Catholic, a substantial proportion of them are estranged from the Catholic Church. In spite of a long association between Mi'kmaw peoples and the Catholic Church dating to earliest fur trade alliances at the turn of the seventeenth century, a crucial rupture occurred in the twentieth century as a result of a partnership of the church and the federal government that produced the Indian residential school system. In Nova Scotia, the Shubenacadie School (which was operated by the Sisters of Charity and the Roman Catholic Diocese of Halifax), was the church's and government's chief agent of cultural assault upon the Mi'kmaq. One of seventy-seven similar institutions across Canada, Shubenacadie was in operation from 1930 to 1967, during which time two thousand Mi'kmaw children were systematically stripped of their language, subjected to abuse, refused proper medical care, and denied filial relationships.[56] "There we learned hatred for one another," writes the poet Helen Sylliboy:

no one knew our Indian names
no one was in truth a sister or brother
no one was allowed to play games

we were taught we were stupid lazy
not allowed to speak our native tongue
some stayed sane others went crazy
some stayed awhile some stayed too long

we prayed from dawn till dusk
did our penance for things so small
were kept like animals in a park
fed cleaned trained no love at all

we forgot the teachings of our people
the ways of our elders the l'nu way
we learned to hate the steeple
a symbol of the abuse day by day.[57]

The long-term results of the residential schools have been devastating: they include widespread loss of the Mi'kmaw language, various kinds of emotional problems, violence, and the devaluation of Mi'kmaw knowledge. The legacy of this experience permeates the community and is expressed in a current epidemic of social illnesses of all forms, including suicide—reverberations of what is called Shubenacadie School syndrome by some. The mechanisms in place for dealing with these devastating problems are not working. They are too often administered by non-Natives, or in some instances by Mi'kmaq who have been thoroughly educated in dominant models of psychotherapy, counseling, medicine, and the sciences broadly and who have inherited a deep suspicion of knowledge systems identified as Mi'kmaq. That they are not working is an understatement. Studies have shown, for example, that First Nations youths are at a much higher risk for committing suicide than are their non-Native counterparts. The suicide rate among young Native men is five times that of non-Natives, and among girls, the rate is eight times higher. Depression, not surprisingly, has been identified as the principle predictor of suicidal tendencies, and among Mi'kmaq between the ages of twelve and eighteen, 25 percent of boys and almost 50 percent of girls have been shown to suffer from depression.[58]

Another tragic illustration of the community's deep malaise occurred a few years after my initial Kluskap conversations, when Nora Bernard was brutally murdered in December 2007. Mrs. Bernard was a Mi'kmaw elder who had spent fifteen years advocating for payment of compensation to those who had been subjected to residential school education. The murder was linked to drug abuse problems in her community. A champion of First Nations rights, she had launched the first class action lawsuit against the government of Canada for its culpability in the abuses suffered by Native children. A parallel suit later launched in Ontario united with that of Mrs. Bernard, and in 2006 First Nations people represented in the suit achieved Canada's largest ever class action settlement—somewhere between four and five billion dollars.[59] It was a bitter irony that a woman who had labored on behalf of the survivors of the residential school system (and had survived that trauma herself) should have ultimately fallen victim to the legacy of illness unleashed by the schools.

Shubenacadie School syndrome is one in a range of deeply embedded problems that are rooted in three centuries of colonial oppression. Integrated Science was part of a new mode of confronting these problems. Ultimately, however, the program would not fully live up to the hopes of its original designers. Within a few years it became obvious that Integrated Science would be dominated by a Western scientific model, with the role of Mi'kmaw knowledge reduced to an addendum (for example, the addition of a unit on Mi'kmaw medicines) and the Mi'kmaw language being used primarily to translate non-Native course content. At the time when the architects of the program and I spoke, however, the program looked as though it might be part of a different kind of approach to the problems plaguing the community, one that had begun most graphically with a Supreme Court of Canada holding in the case of *R v. Marshall* (1999).

By virtue of the treaties of 1760 and 1761, which were entered into by the Mi'kmaq and the British Crown, the Mi'kmaq (who have the smallest reserve land base in Canada) were granted the right to catch and sell fish.[60] These rights were constantly denied during the Canadian period until 1985, when James Simon won the right to hunt for food anywhere in Mi'kmakik (the lands of the Mi'kmaq), thereby winning limited recognition of the validity of the so-called Friendship Treaties.[61] A subsequent decision, however, had farther-reaching implications. In the mid-1990s, Donald Marshall was found guilty in the Nova Scotia Court of Appeal of fishing eels out of season, of fishing without a license, and of fishing with an illegal net (by implication, for sale). A team of lawyers (four of whom were Mi'kmaq) took the case to the Supreme Court, and in September of 1999 the Court upheld Marshall's right to catch and sell fish in accordance with the treaties of 1760 and 1761.[62] The young Mi'kmaw lawyers involved in the case used their legal training, their knowledge of the Canadian judicial system, and their understandings of the treaties to take on the system in its highest court. For many, their method became a model for confronting the legacy of colonialism, and those with whom I spoke on my Kluskap journey envisioned Toqwa'tu'kl Kjijitaqnn in these terms: as a program whose intention it was to use the language, methods, and knowledge base of Western science, as well as the structure of the academy, to assert the validity of Mi'kmaw meanings of the environment and to incorporate them into the management of the natural environment and human illness for the benefit of the land and the Mi'kmaw people.

Over the span of my initial Kluskap journey, I heard a great deal about treaty rights, residential schools, and aquatic parasites. I never got a Kluskap story, but I did discover *Alpha* in a new way. I found myself pouring over the final pages of the book, in which Long confronted us in 1962 with the arduous task of seeing clearly our modern cultural situation and opening our ears to the new myths that will order and humanize the world that is coming into being. In light of these pages, retreating into *Alpha* as I had initially and simplistically intended—as though it could provide a catchall template for accounting for Kluskap myths—became impossible, except perhaps in a much more broad sense. For human communities, Long wrote, the discovery of new cultural dimensions coincides with new dimensions of being, and myths have allowed humans to respond to these new modes of being. These structures have represented both a confrontation with the world and a conceptual means of grasping it. Given that myths express a human response to the advent of new cultural dimensions, Long asked, "What new structures will inform the modern period?" and he raised the prospect in 1962 that science and technology would have a substantive role in the definition of our modern situation.[63] Looking to the Mi'kmaq, there is no doubt that science and technology occupy a critical position, but sustained autocratic regulation must also be counted as among the dominant cultural structures of the period (as applied through education, government policy, and law).

As I attempted to find the way in which illness, suicide, diseased oysters, new science, the sale of fish, and the Milky Way related to one another, I recalled a line in *Alpha*. "It is impossible," wrote Long, "to understand the

reality and being of [a] people, unless one understands their reality in relation to the myth."[64] It occurred to me then that I had indeed heard a story
from one of my friends, told to me after we had discussed *Alpha* at some
length. At the time, I thought it had little relevance for my broader concern
with Kluskap and the modernization of myth, but as I later grappled with
those days of discussion, they came together in some manner in relation to
this myth. The story went roughly like this:

> In the 1920s at Antigonish, Nova Scotia, there was a woman who had
> seven children, by seven different men. She never married. She was
> very spiritual and considered by her community also to be very holy.
> The woman was hardworking. She fed, clothed, and cared for her
> seven children to adulthood.
>
> Throughout her adult life, the parish priest cited her as an example
> of depravity. He saw her as immoral and lascivious, and when she
> eventually died, the priest refused to allow her to be buried in the
> church cemetery. He did not want her body placed in consecrated
> ground. The cemetery was located on the top of a knoll, and the
> ground dropped off beyond the knoll into a ravine.
>
> The women's children pleaded with the priest to bury their mother
> in the church cemetery, to no avail. Following her funeral, she was
> taken beyond church property to the bottom of the ravine and buried
> there. It was almost dark when the priest left, and the children con-
> ducted their own traditional ceremony (*salite*), following which they
> turned for home. The sky behind them began to glow, and looking
> back toward the burial place, they saw lights dancing in the darkness.
> Turning back toward the lights, they followed them back to the place
> where their mother was buried at the bottom of the ravine. These
> lights were not coming from the sky, but from seven beings stand-
> ing around the new grave, and who were sending up seven beams
> of light.
>
> One of the children went to get the priest, who resisted but finally
> followed her back to the gravesite. Upon seeing the beings, he
> dropped to his knees, head in hands, and began to weep and ask for
> forgiveness. The beings informed him that this woman was special
> and holy and that his treatment of her was sacrilegious. They told
> the priest that she should be moved from the ravine to be reburied
> up on the hill in consecrated ground. He said he would do so, but to
> make certain that he would fulfill his promise he was told that the

seven beings would remain all night with the woman and watch him remove her at dawn. At sunrise, he unearthed the woman's body and carried her up the hill where he reburied her in the church cemetery.

The colonial and postcolonial worlds of the Mi'kmaq have been characterized by alienation from land, by cultural assault, and by rampant illness of all forms, and this community has had little efficacy in arresting this cycle of destruction. There has been a totality of chaos at the foundation of the modern Mi'kmaw world, and the chaos within this New World is reminiscent, in its latent possibilities, of that at the root of many originary myths about which we read in *Alpha*—myths of World Parents, or a united earth and sky, in which offspring exist in darkness as no more than potentialities, and in which the union must be ruptured for both offspring and an ordered world to come into existence. Within the chaos that characterizes the unilateral power relations of the myth from Antigonish, the seven offspring require just such a rupture for their voices to be heard. In both cases, light enacts the separation that heralds a new order within which these offspring become agents rather than shadows.[65]

Long wrote toward the end of *Alpha* that myth can be used as a tool for historical research; he then considered the question of whether myth can be a "mode of orientation in the modern period."[66] As a tool for understanding, the power of myth cannot be overestimated. In the myth at Antigonish, I was afforded a glimpse of the meaning of what had previously appeared to be rather arbitrary discussions. Broken treaties and institutionalized abuse of children resonated metaphorically with the priest at the top of the hill, while disease and silence were the inheritances of the offspring of this chaos. Redemption from chaos was possible only by means of an impetus from the earth far below, with which the people shared a sacred relationship. As Albert said to me, only the Mi'kmaq appear capable of understanding, and tending to, the welfare of an oyster.[67] As the first rays of light broke through the darkness, order began to be restored and, within that order, the silent oppressed were able to overtake the space from which chaos emanated—a cemetery, the Supreme Court, or the academy. As a microcosm, the myth is perhaps a sacred model of a Mi'kmaw world that may yet come into being within the parameters of modernity and, as such, represents a significant mode by which myth can be a medium of orientation in the modern period.

2

KLUSKAP AND ABORIGINAL RIGHTS

For months after I had completed my presentation at the American Academy of Religion meeting, I was haunted by the elusive figure who had been standing in the background throughout. It seemed to me for a while that my search for contemporary Kluskap stories had been a fruitless exercise. I had spent a good part of a summer looking for stories, but those with whom I spoke never really got around to telling me any. In every case, what looked to be a preamble to a story became the focus of our conversation. Often when I asked for a story, I was told that Kluskap was a figure who was associated with landscape. But rather than hearing a story, I heard about aquatic parasites and oysters, broken treaties, aspirations for the study of science, and the Supreme Court of Canada. I concluded at the time that the myths simply were not being told any more, and I started to wonder if perhaps they had never been as important as earlier non-Native writers would have had us believe. But something about all this immediately seemed wrong. First, although the stories had undoubtedly been colored by the people who recorded them, these writers had nonetheless heard them from actual people. Some, like Rand and the Wallises, provided broad citations for their myths. Others, however, were much more meticulous in giving credit to those who had shared them. Speck's myths, for example, came from a number of persons whom Speck named; and those whom I have cited in this book were given to him by Chief Joe Julian of Sydney and John Joe of Whycocomagh in the early 1920s. Arthur Fauset collected stories from a number of Mi'kmaq living in Laquille, near Annapolis Royal, in 1923; and Elsie Clews Parsons specifically credited those who had shared stories with her in the 1920s: Isabelle Googoo Morris (Whycocomaugh), Mary Madeline Newall Poulet (Chapel Island), and Lucy Pictou (Laquille).[1] It started to occur to me that the salient issue might not be the exaggerations of earlier folklorists, missionaries, and ethnographers but the relationship between what appears to have been an earlier interest in the telling of Kluskap stories of some form or another and the more recent ebbing of interest in doing so. This shift in focus would ultimately lead me to an appreciation of Kluskap as a figure who is indelibly linked to a series of eighteenth-century treaties negotiated by the Mi'kmaq and the British government. But I am getting ahead of myself. At that moment, my interest was in understanding the apparently dwindling interest in telling these stories.

A number of explanations for the earlier popularity of Kluskap myths have been suggested. They have been said to have embodied "laws, morals, and wisdom" that were necessary for the survival of the Mi'kmaw people;[2] to have made the natural and social landscapes "intelligible"; and to have provided "mental shelter" and comfort during times of difficulty, especially during the nineteenth century, when annihilation of the Mi'kmaq seemed to be looming.[3] There is undoubtedly truth in all these explanations, but they provide only a part of Kluskap's morphology. Comfort, obviously, was necessary in the nineteenth century, as the Mi'kmaq faced loss of land, rampant disease, and starvation of unprecedented magnitude. Beginning at the turn of the nineteenth century, encroachment on Aboriginal lands became widespread and unrestrained. In 1783, for example, a New Brunswick band obtained a license of occupation from the government of Nova Scotia for twenty thousand acres along the Miramichi River.[4] Between 1785 and 1807 the band repeatedly requested that the license be confirmed in the face of excessive encroachment by non-Native settlers, and the result of their continued effort was the establishment of a land reserve in 1807. The reserve, however, was half the size specified in the original license. During the same period, another Mi'kmaw community was granted four thousand acres of land on the eastern side of the Wagamatcook River in Cape Breton Island. By the 1860s, all that was left of the tract was seven hundred acres containing a village, a burial ground, and a grove of sugar maples.[5] Along with encroachment, the Mi'kmaq had to contend with unparalleled deprivation and disease during the period. In 1831, for example, Mi'kmaq at Rawden, Nova Scotia, possessed ten blankets for fifty people, and in 1834, those of Windsor were without adequate clothing and shelter. In the 1840s and 1850s, Mi'kmaq throughout Nova Scotia and Cape Breton Island were dying of starvation, while measles, whooping cough, scarlet fever, croup, typhus, and small pox were so rampant that deaths were occurring daily in some communities.[6] There is no doubt that Kluskap myths could have functioned as a form of consolation in this situation. After all, there was a vein of incredible hospitality running through the myths of the period. Reflecting on the "quiet humor" that characterized the hero, for example, Elder wrote in 1871, "One can fairly detect a smile in his eyes, as he sees the glum looks of his disappointed guests, when, instead of the savory meat of the moose or caribou, the old woman brings out a dried beaver bone, and scrapes a little of it in the pot, and prepares it for their supper, and share his enjoyment of their surprise, when they find the dish set before them to be so delicious that they can scarcely stop eating."[7]

The quality of the food that Kluskap served to those who came to him was a common motif in the stories, but more striking still was that of its quantity. Many writers recorded myths in which endless supplies of food were produced from nothing more than a simple shard of bone. In Rand, we read of two hungry young men who visited Kluskap and were handed a dish of food that was so meager they were utterly dispirited. However, their moods soon improved. "Small as is the portion of food assigned to them, they may eat as much as they like, but they cannot reduce the amount; there is just as much in the dish as ever. They finish their meal, and are well satisfied and refreshed."[8] Another, similar story from the turn of the century provides more detail:

> One time Edunabes' was short on food. He said, "I'm going to visit Gluskap, perhaps I'll get some food there. I'm going tonight." He started to walk early in the morning. Late in the evening he got there. Gluskap was glad to see his friend. "You have come," he said. "Yes. I have come to see you." Gluskap said to his grandmother, "Cook something for him." She said, "I'll cook some soup for him." — She had only one little pot. Edunabes' said, "That pot I'll finish in no time." The old lady cooked that much and she put her hand under the boughs and brought out a bark cup and two bark spoons. She said, "Take your soup." They finished their plates. Gluskap said, "Grand-mother, put in a little more." — "All right," she said. She put in a little more. They ate that. She put in a little more. They ate that. The little pot kept filling up. The old lady got tired serving those fellows. She told Marten to wait on them. She said, "I'm going to sleep." Marten

put some more in for them until early in the morning he got tired. Then Gluskap himself took the spoon and kept giving food to his visitor until nearly daybreak. "Oh, I guess that's plenty," he said, "belly has not been filled for some time.[9]

We can hear variations of the story also in Lonecloud's conversations with Dennis in the 1920s:

> While the water was boiling, he put his hand behind him. He was sitting on some brush. He hauled out a little bone, which he scraped into the pot. When they looked, where there was water a few minutes ago, now was fat moose meat. He found another bone, and when another pot was boiling, he scraped in that also. All looked closely, and in an instant, it was filled with fat bear meat. A third time he hauled a bone and scraped it into a pot and put it back, and in a twinkling of an eye, was fat beaver meat where before was water. . . . They had a great feast.[10]

Lonecloud also attributed to Kluskap the ability to make a single moose feed far more people than was possible: "Some knew that if Glooscap handed it out they would all get a piece; others doubted. However all obtained a piece."[11] For communities in which people were suffering privation, going without proper food, and at times dying of starvation, stories of a hero who could produce endless supplies of delicious food from nothing could well have provided a sense of comfort. But I think there is more to these stories than that; and in regarding them merely as psychological analgesics, we may be overlooking another salient aspect of their morphology: their capacity to represent Mi'kmaw interests in what was a protracted contest over the significance of eighteenth-century treaties and the nature of the relationship between Mi'kmaw and non-Native populations.

Recent scholars have claimed that Kluskap myths were recorded as early as the eighteenth century[12] and that these stories were unequivocally part of an oral culture that predates contact with Europeans.[13] While they may indeed have a primordial structure, what we can say with certainty is that the myths in which Kluskap figured gained noticeable momentum in the mid-nineteenth century. Although numerous Catholic missionaries since the turn of the sixteenth century had gone to great lengths to describe what they regarded as the religious world of the Mi'kmaq, no reference to the hero appears in any of the early *Jesuit Relations* or later eighteenth-century missionary correspondences.[14] Written records of Kluskap appear for the first time at the point when the Mi'kmaq were facing possible annihilation. There is no doubt that these recorded myths were riddled with non-Native elements, but there were also striking common elements that were present throughout the various stories that do not appear to have been non-Native fabrications. Prominent among these elements were (1) Kluskap's role in the creation of the natural landscape and (2) his authority to situate both the Mi'kmaw and non-Native populations primordially within that landscape.

In these stories, Kluskap was responsible for the creation of landscape features throughout Quebec, New Brunswick, Nova Scotia, and Cape Breton Island.[15] His kettle was an island;[16] his canoe was a large rock;[17] and his dogs, at his departure, were turned to stone.[18] He created turtles, tadpoles, crabs, and leeches;[19] took the noses from porcupines and toads;[20] gave beavers their tails; gave frogs and loons their distinctive voices;[21] and reduced all the animals to the sizes they now are. "Glous'gap created the animals, and as he called each to him, he gave it a name. He made the squirrel and named him A'dou'dou'gwetj, or Chatter. That squirrel was as big as a whale! 'What will you do if I let you loose on the world'? Glous'gap asked A'dou'dou'gwetj. With that the squirrel leaped over to a towering tree and brought it down with a crash. 'You're too destructive to be so big'! Glous'gap scolded as he reshaped A'dou'dou'gwetj into the little fellow he remains today."[22]

He left his footprints in stone,[23] cleared rivers for navigation,[24] carved channels with his paddle,[25] gave names to the principle places along the shorelines of the Maritime Provinces, and finally, named all the stars and constellations.[26] The natural environment was a theater in which Kluskap helped to create a world; and in that world he gave the Mi'kmaq primordial rights to harvesting of various types. He was, primarily, a teacher. As Rand put it, "All that the Indians knew of what was wise and good he taught them."[27] He taught them the names of the stars and how to build canoes, but most often in the stories, he taught the Mi'kmaq how to hunt, fish, and cure what they harvested and how to find medicines to heal sickness.[28] The myths were unmistakably woven around a motif involving a relationship between Kluskap, the landscape, and the Mi'kmaq as harvesters, a relationship that was described explicitly to Wallis in 1911:

> Gluskap taught our people to make bows, arrows, fishhooks, and stone pipes, and showed the Micmac how to fish, hunt, and make a living, and also what to procure as medicines. He was born in the

same way as any of us. He must have been a leader among his people, the Old Indians said, because he knew everything so well. Gluskap said, "You are now free to get your living where you like. But there will come a day when you will be prevented" (referring to the game laws and property of the English settlers and present inhabitants). He was correct. Now we may not go out and kill moose and partridge.[29]

To this theme of a primordial relationship between Kluskap, the people, and the land we must add that of the foundational presence of non-Native peoples. As I mentioned earlier, the arrival of colonial Europeans was given an originary meaning through various prophesies of European incursion that we hear in these myths. In addition, there are stories in which Christianity and both the British and French monarchies are present as cultural forms with which Kluskap contends prior to Europeans' invasion of North America. Speck, for example, recorded a story of an ancient confrontation between Kluskap and Christ, in which Christ was concerned with testing Kluskap's power. "He took Gluskap to the ocean, and told him to close his eyes. Then Christ moved close to the shore an island that lay far out to sea. When Gluskap opened his eyes, he saw it. Christ asked him if he could do as much as that. Then Gluskap told Christ to close his eyes a while. When Christ opened his eyes, he found that Gluskap had moved it back to its place again."[30]

In another, more elaborate story that Wallis heard from a man named Peter Ginnish in 1911, Kluskap traveled across the Atlantic before the British and French knew of North America. The myth strikingly foreshadows the Mi'kmaw people's relationship with both colonial powers. Early fur trade relationships dating to the late sixteenth and early seventeenth centuries, along with intermarriage, conversion to Catholicism, and military alliances, ensured that the Mi'kmaq had traditionally enjoyed much more cordial relations with the French than with the British. According to this myth, the nature of these relationships had been determined well before contact, when Kluskap traveled across the ocean in the mouth of a whale, moving onto a small island as he reached England.

It was the first island the English people had ever seen, and they thought it was very pretty. It contained woods and trees so high that only with difficulty could they see to the top of them. The king ordered a man to try to find the man who was in charge there. A ship was sent out, and a boat from it went to the shore of the island. They found a man there and asked him, "Where are you from?" "I am from out there," said Gluskap, pointing westward. "Do you intend to remain here?" "To be sure, I shall stay here."

. . . The captain went ashore and said to him, "Come aboard; the King wishes to see you. We will put you ashore." "No; go back; tomorrow morning I shall be there." They reported his words to the King. On the following morning it was found that the island was close to the shore. The King told Gluskap to come ashore. "I am not ready to go yet," said Gluskap; "I shall go when I am ready." The King threatened to kill him when he did come ashore.

Accordingly, the King built a big pile of wood and had ready for use a large flask of oil. Gluskap went ashore, and all the while kept very quiet. Two officers took him, handcuffed him, and put him on the pile of wood. Fire was placed to it. It blazed high, and finally the pile was burned to the bottom. When it had burned out, Gluskap was found sitting in the midst of it, just as they had placed him, smoking his pipe. The King saw him and was frightened. Those who were standing by said, "We must kill that man now." They rammed powder into a canon and put him in as a wad. The canon was fired off; Gluskap walked out and asked, "Where is the King?" The King was called. He went to Gluskap and wished to shake hands with him. Gluskap said, "I cannot touch your hand, for it is of no account—it is like yourself. You, too, are no good; you are a very hardhearted man. When you called me from out there, I thought you would accord me better treatment than I have received. You have treated me very badly. . . ."

The King then knelt before him. "Get up," said Gluskap; "I don't want that. But do not treat people in such manner as you have treated me, for you do not know whom you may encounter. You may be the Master of this World, but there is another who is Master over you. I shall leave you now. If I had not shown myself more powerful than you, you would have killed me . . ." The King told his sailors to take the man to his palace. "No; I do not want any of you or any of your people near me. Your people are of no account—they are not trustworthy. If I were not able to withstand you, I should now be a dead man. However, you have had your last opportunity to injure me."

When he left them, he got into no boat, but walked on the water, as though it were a floor, went over it to his island, and remained there during the rest of the day. Next morning he went to France on his island. France had heard of this island—Silver Island. The French then had a King. The King dressed, and went on a boat to the island. There he saw Gluskap's wigwam and saw smoke coming from it. Gluskap knew the King was coming . . . When the King came to the entrance, Gluskap rose and went to the door. The King offered his hand.

Gluskap took it, and said, "Come in. Take a seat." The King did not understand, for this was spoken in Micmac. Gluskap, however, understood all languages.

The King of France invited Gluskap to his palace. "Oh no; I can't go there. . . . I have already called on one King, who treated me very badly, and I think you, too, would treat me that way. I came here merely to see your country. I shall not return until the time comes." He did not explain what time he meant. The King said, "I should be very much pleased if you would come and see my country." Gluskap said to him, "I do see your country. It is very nice. But within your palace all is not well. If you are not careful, you will not retain your power; I can see as much from here." The King, when he heard this, almost fell down, and could not reply.

There is now no King in France.[31]

There were obviously many variations in the Kluskap myths we have been considering here. Nonetheless, there were a number of unmistakably common features in the stories, too. These include (1) Kluskap's role in the creation of the Mi'kmaw world, (2) the situation of the Mi'kmaq as harvesters in that world, and (3) the primordial meaning of colonial contact. As I thought about these commonalities, it began to occur to me that they seemed to relate to the treaties that were negotiated by the Mi'kmaq and the British in the eighteenth century. Evidence to support this suggestion is found not only in the content of the stories but also in the fact that the period during which they were apparently being often repeated coincides precisely with the time frame during which these treaties were being utterly disregarded by governing bodies in Canada. Kluskap may well have related quite specifically to this situation.

The Mi'kmaq negotiated their first treaty with the British government in 1726, and this treaty became the basis for a series of other agreements. The 1726 treaty was an exchange of promises of friendship between the Mi'kmaq and British settlers, and, critically, it recognized the Mi'kmaw right to harvest on the land they occupied, as well as the right to pursue other necessary activities (presumably, although not explicitly stated, collecting herbs and firewood and using the rivers to travel inland in winter). The actual territory they inhabited was not specified, but the assumption was that it included lands not occupied by colonial settlers.[32] The treaty thus limited the amount of land that was available for settlers, effectively checking colonial expansion. The intent of the agreement was to define the kinds of actions that would promote peaceful relations between colonials and Native peoples. Essentially, neither community was permitted to infringe on the territory inhabited by the other, and the Mi'kmaq agreed to recognize the legitimacy of British law in instances where conflicts arose between the two communities.[33] Occupation of harvesting territory was a fundamental part of the treaty of 1726, which was renegotiated in 1749 and 1752 and reaffirmed again in 1760 and 1761. By the 1752 accord, the Mi'kmaq consented to mutual use of the land with British settlers, but they did not surrender the land itself. Delegates from the community agreed to attend annual meetings with representatives of the Crown, to respect colonial settlements, and to maintain trade solely with the British. In return, the British government promised to protect their harvesting rights and to provide truck houses (trading posts) and, periodically, certain necessities like blankets and corn. The Mi'kmaq were thus able to continue their established subsistence practices, harvesting in designated areas that were located at a distance from colonial settlements.

In spite of these treaties, a French-Native alliance resisted full British sovereignty in Acadia until midcentury, when the expulsion of the Acadians in 1755 and the French losses of Fort Beauséjour and Louisbourg in 1757 and 1758, respectively, signaled the end of the alliance. To formalize the resolution of British-Mi'kmaw hostility a series of treaties were negotiated, and ten such treaties were signed with the Mi'kmaq in 1760 and 1761. The treaties were not unequivocal in many respects (especially regarding the issue of land ownership), but they were very clear in terms of guaranteeing Native peoples the right to continued use of natural resources. During this period, the British were clearly attentive to the possibility of encroachment on Native land; and in 1763, the British government issued a royal proclamation that asserted its sovereignty over the region but stipulated that Aboriginal lands could not be infringed upon unless a treaty had been negotiated. Relying on customary colonial practice based on the doctrine of discovery (one of the oldest principles of international law), the Crown prohibited all negotiations relating to the sale of Aboriginal land, reserving this prerogative to itself: any land that was not already settled by Europeans was to be reserved for the use of Native peoples and could not be used otherwise without the negotiation of a treaty.[34] In so doing, the British government separated the issue of sovereignty (which it claimed over the region) from the business of surrendering title to the land. Although the proclamation did not ultimately result in fair treatment for the Mi'kmaq, its ostensible intention had been to protect them from appropriation and to maintain land for their use while asserting Britain's underlying title to their land.[35]

The inherently conflicted nature of the treaty-making process, however, has had long-term repercussions. William Wicken has argued that the need for treaties reflected a changing demographic, through which the colonial British and Mi'kmaw communities came to find themselves sharing a territory in which the space between them was diminishing. The process was a clear indication that the British regarded peaceful relations with the Mi'kmaq as a necessity and that they expected the Mi'kmaq to be active participants in drafting the guidelines that would regulate the actions of both groups as they shared this shrinking space. The Mi'kmaq, then, occupied a very different position from that of the Acadians, whom the British had chosen to deport from the region. By entering into negotiations, the British recognized the Mi'kmaq as a politically legitimate and independent body; and this assumption is what lies behind the fact that no subsequent attempts were made to restrict or influence the political or social structure of the Mi'kmaw nation during the colonial period (this would change dramatically in the post-1867 Canadian period). In effect, there was an assumption of reciprocity in the nature of the treaty-making process. At the same time, however, references to Mi'kmaw capitulation to British authority, as it was expressed in the treaties, contradicted the logic underlying the act of negotiation, insofar as that process assumed a degree of agency on the part of both parties. As Wicken notes, this process "silenced Mi'kmaq voices while simultaneously privileging those voices."[36]

This original anomaly would become amplified in the years following the period of treaty making, as Mi'kmaw and non-Native populations developed dramatically different understandings of the meaning of the agreements. It is important to note that these were peace treaties, and so were unlike their counterparts in the Canadian west, insofar as they did not deal with the issue of forfeiting resources. In spite of this, the non-Native claim that the treaties somehow constituted a Mi'kmaw submission to British law and, consequently, a surrender of land claims, has been argued in the courts to the present day. The Mi'kmaq, on the other hand, have maintained a vision of the treaties as "peace accords"—legal agreements to refrain from warfare and to share the region's resource base. This perception was confirmed during the first few decades following the ratification of these agreements, a period marked by a relatively unaltered situation for the Mi'kmaq in terms of resource use.[37] The nineteenth century, however, changed this situation dramatically.

These treaties dealt with two categories of rights that would later be specified in the Canadian Constitution Act of 1982: (1) Aboriginal rights based on "prior occupation" of the continent (rights not held by non-Natives) and (2) treaty rights based on the text of such agreements, and in the case of the Mi'kmaq, presumably pertaining to harvesting.[38] In the nineteenth and early twentieth centuries, while both forms of rights were being consistently denied and the Mi'kmaw community was consequently undergoing devastation, the Mi'kmaq sought redress from colonial and British governments and, later, Canadian courts. Reminding the British government that Mi'kmaw allegiance to the British Crown, for instance, had been negotiated in exchange for recognition of Aboriginal and treaty rights, the Mi'kmaq of Burnt Church, Nova Scotia, petitioned the home government in the 1840s, writing that the Mi'kmaq "have never broken their word, but have been true and Loyal Subjects and therefore trust that you the Representatives of their Great Mistress the Queen will never consent to break their Location or abridge their privileges in any manner whatever."[39]

In 1867, when the provinces of Nova Scotia and New Brunswick entered into the Canadian Confederation, rumors that the Dominion would not recognize existing treaty rights compelled Peter Cope to travel to the Colonial Office in London to petition on behalf of the Mi'kmaw community. He was assured that all treaty agreements would be honored by the Canadian government, which was to have jurisdiction over Indian affairs.[40]

Canadian Aboriginal rights were dealt a near lethal blow two decades later, when the *Saint Catherine's Milling Case* of 1888 established that Native peoples did not have recourse to the judicial system in affirming their treaty rights. The case technically involved the federal and Ontario governments, which each claimed to have control over Crown land and resources. The federal government had negotiated Treaty 3 with Ojibwa in the region between the Manitoba border and Lake Superior, but the provincial government argued that Ontario owned the resources on this land. The case was taken to the Privy Council, which held in favor of the province of Ontario, asserting that Aboriginal claims were superseded by the rights of provincial governments. This case ultimately made it impossible for First Nations peoples to use the courts to argue for land claims and treaty rights in the nineteenth century.[41] In fact, even departments of Indian affairs had no interest in addressing this issue. The nineteenth-century historian Luther Roth wrote in 1891 of two Mi'kmaw men, John Barnaby and Alexander Marshall, who traveled to Halifax to meet Indian Affairs officials to file a grievance "in connection with their fisheries in the Restigouche River. They complained that their nets had been seized and their fish taken. But their mission was fruitless, as they had unwittingly come in conflict with the Fisheries and Game Act of the Dominion. The untutored natives do not have almanacs, and if they had would not be able to read them; beside which, not knowing anything about the months, they could not tell when the prohibition against fishing with nets and seines [large vertical weighted nets] was in force."[42]

Another judicial ruling, this time involving the Mi'kmaq directly, drove the point home early in the twentieth century. In *Syliboy* (1928), Grand Chief Gabriel Syliboy appealed his conviction on charges of having been in illegal possession of pelts in contravention of Lands and Forests regulations.[43] He had not actually trapped the animals himself, but as grand chief he assumed responsibility for the pelts so he could defend the treaties in court. Syliboy argued that he had "by Treaty the right to hunt and fish at all times," a claim that had not previously been made by a Native person in a Canadian court. The chief witness in the trial was Antel Alex (Andrew Aleck), who held the position of *putus* (wampum reader) at that time. As putus, Alex was responsible for reading and interpreting the wampum that recorded the treaties. Consequently he was regarded by the Mi'kmaq as an authority on the treaties. His testimony at the trial focused on traditional treaty rights:

> Live on Indian Reserve near Saint Peters. Born there & lived there all my life. I am 78 years old. Mostly fishing. All kinds of fish. Am a Micmac. Micmacs had right to fish all they cd. Eat or sell at all seasons of year. Remember getting gifts from Gov't. When I was ten years old father had a team. No one else had a team. At first went to Sydney for blankets. Father & mother and each child got blanket. Went with my father to Sydney for blankets. Got them from Dodd. Knew him when I saw him. Got coats as well and hide for moccasins. And flour Indian meal gun powder shot. In Spring wd. get seed. Potatoes oats corn and turnip. Nobody ever interfered with our fishing and hunting.[44]

Alex did not claim to have any special insight into the treaties in the context of the trial, although his community understood that he was testifying in his capacity as putus. While the community would have considered his testimony as extremely significant, it was meaningless to the court. In his ruling, presiding judge Patterson claimed that the Treaty of 1752 was not a treaty that applied to the Mi'kmaq of Cape Breton Island. "The Treaty of 1752 made between Governor Hopson and certain of the Mick Mack Indians of Nova Scotia, . . . did not extend to Cape Breton Indians. The latter therefore acquired no rights to hunt under the treaty contrary to the general game laws of Nova Scotia."[45] Sylliboy's conviction was, consequently, affirmed.

During the period in question, the Mi'kmaq (and indeed all First Nations peoples in Canada) had no means by which to create a discourse about their treaty and Aboriginal rights with non-Native governing and judicial bodies. Moreover, the period coincides directly with that during which Kluskap myths were recorded with greatest vigor. These myths, told to non-Native writers, may well have been a sacred language about treaties. Like the treaties, the myths asserted rights of occupation and harvesting; but going further, they located these rights in a primordium that conceded both the incursion of Europeans and the reality of new relationships based on this social transformation. The treaties themselves have been traditionally regarded as sacred documents. The Kluskap myths, in concert with the eighteenth-century treaties, articulated a relationship between the Mi'kmaq and non-Natives that was based on acknowledgment of the coexistence of two distinct and autonomous communities, as well as on the Mi'kmaw people's primary occupation and subsistence association with the land. Subsequent disregard of these legal agreements by both colonial governments and the Canadian and British judiciaries created a conflict regarding the spatial foundation of the new Canadian society. For non-Natives, First Nations' submission to the British Crown signaled the surrender of land and resource claims. For the Mi'kmaq, submission constituted an agreement to share resources, based upon the British government's recognition of occupation and harvesting rights. During the nineteenth and early twentieth centuries, Kluskap myths appear to have maintained a discursive Mi'kmaw foothold in an epistemological and legal contest over the rights of Native peoples in an emerging postcolonial state, a contest that non-Natives refused to acknowledge. In other words, within the Kluskap myths was encoded the primary text of the treaties—recognition of Mi'kmaw occupation and harvesting rights in Maritime Canada.

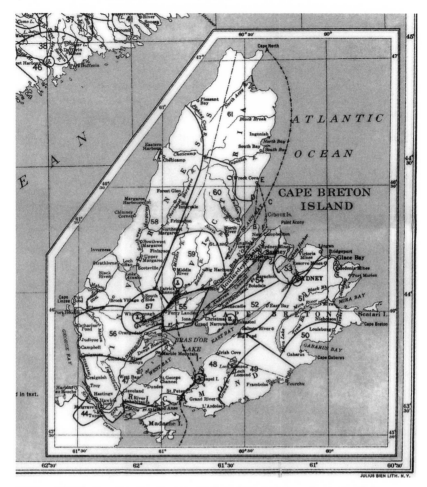

Map 1   Detail of mythic hunting territories of Cape Breton. From Frank G.
Speck, *Beothuk and Micmac* (New York: Museum of the American Indian, Heye
Foundation, 1922).

To add some weight to this argument, I would like to consider a map
that Frank Speck included in his 1922 book, *Beothuk and Micmac* (map 1).
The map portrayed all major communities (non-Native and Mi'kmaq) as
they existed on Cape Breton Island in 1922. In addition to this, Speck
had drawn a series of "hunting territories" that had been mentioned in a
body of Kluskap stories he had collected in the early part of the twentieth
century. The map thus represented Cape Breton Island's communities in
the early 1920s, while depicting a group of mythic "hunting territories"
that were nonexistent during that time. When, however, we turn to a map
from the period immediately following that during which the treaties were

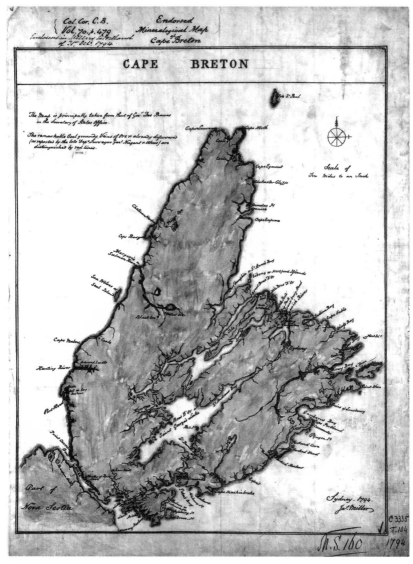

Map 2   Cape Breton, ca. 1794, by Joseph Miller. Library and Archives Canada/
NMC 161.

negotiated, something interesting becomes apparent. Map 2 shows the
principal settlements on Cape Breton Island in the late eighteenth century.
When Speck's hunting territories are overlaid on the eighteenth-century
map, we can see a curious social and spatial arrangement (map 3).

Essentially, the Mi'kmaw hunting territories delineated in early twentieth-
century myths and the colonial settlements on the eighteenth-century map

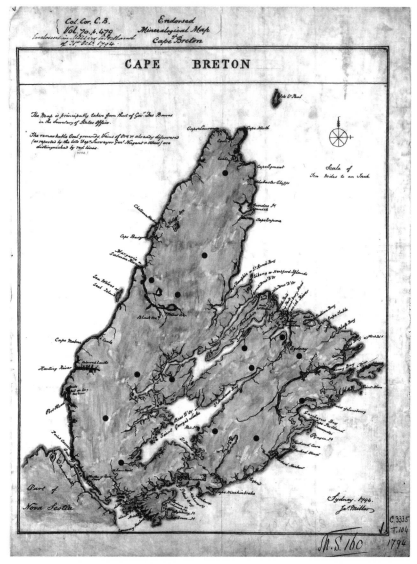

Map 3   Composite map showing locations of hunting territories and colonial
settlements

are no less than about fifty miles apart in any instance. If the eighteenth-
century treaties established the principle that neither community was permitted to infringe on the territory inhabited by the other, then the Mi'kmaw
interpretation of these documents as agreements to share the island's
resources based on a recognition of occupation and harvesting rights
seems to be reflected by the spatial arrangement evident in this overlay.

Moreover, this understanding of the treaties appears to have been embedded in a tradition of myths that were recorded a century and a half after the treaties were negotiated.

This all begs the question, If these myths allowed for a consistent discourse about the eighteenth-century treaties, why has there been an apparent waning of interest in telling them during the past few decades? There is no doubt that Kluskap continues to be a well-known figure whose associations with landscape and creation have remained solid to the present. Still, many of his stories are no longer told to the same degree that they were in the past. Obviously, it would be foolhardy for me to try to explain this shift too easily. There are undoubtedly many contributing factors here. Whitehead, for instance, has suggested that a widespread decline in the telling of mythic stories of all sorts was caused by an increase in reading books in English at the end of the nineteenth century and, subsequently, by the introduction of radio and television (and, we might add here, more recently the social Internet) in the decades that followed. As a consequence, even stories that were recorded during the period became progressively shorter.[46] While I am inclined to agree with Whitehead's argument pointing to various media as contributing factors, the evidence she cites is not unequivocal. Speaking of the Ki'Kwa'ju (Badger) story cycle as evidence of the process, for instance, she points out that it accounts for thirty pages of Rand's 1894 collection, while Wallis's version, based on stories he collected in 1911, filled only eight pages.[47] Although she is correct in terms of the page lengths of these myths, her recourse to this as evidence of the impact of various media is not altogether convincing. An equally plausible explanation might be that Rand began studying the Mi'kmaw language and living among Mi'kmaw peoples in 1846, and he published *Legends of the Micmacs* in 1894. Wallis, on the other hand, spent only two summers collecting stories in the early twentieth century. In this case, at least, it is pretty obvious that Rand simply had time to gather more material than had Wallis.[48]

Still, there is little doubt that the introduction of a variety of new media (especially electronic) has had a negative impact on traditions of storytelling. Additionally—and to my mind, more critically—the cultural effects of the residential school experience must be considered in this situation. The emotional and physical abuse to which children were subjected for decades was part of the government and church's expressed aim of eradicating the Mi'kmaw language. Isabel Knockwood's exposé of life at Shubenacadie School, *Out of the Depths*, contains many passages that deal with this issue. She relates:

Although many of those who so relentlessly punished the children entrusted to them are now dead, the effect of their savage punishments has outlived them. Not only were little children brutally punished for speaking their mother tongue, reducing them to years of speechlessness, but the Mi'kmaw language was constantly referred to as "mumbo jumbo" as if it were some form of gibberish. The ruthless banning of Mi'kmaw in the school drove a wedge between family members. Freda Simon, for example, remembers that when she arrived at the school two years after her older sister they were completely unable to communicate with each other since Freda spoke only Mi'kmaw and her sister spoke only English. The punishment for speaking Mi'kmaw began on our first day at school, but the punishment has continued all our lives as we try to piece together who we are and what the world means to us with a language many of us have had to re-learn as adults.[49]

The dual assault on language and family relationships that occurred at Shubenacadie has had, as I noted earlier, devastating effects on the community. Among these we can safely count the eclipse of various kinds of narrative forms.

This being said, I want to suggest yet another contributing factor that relates to Kluskap: the state of Aboriginal and treaty rights in Canada in the later part of the twentieth century. What I want to suggest here is that discussions about Native rights entered into a different phase in recent decades for which a good part of the past work performed by the telling of Kluskap myths has not been as necessary as it once was. The most recent generation of Mi'kmaq has come of age during the first period since the treaties were negotiated in which treaty and Aboriginal rights are part of a national discourse. Incrementally, but undeniably, these rights are being adjudicated in the Canadian courts, and the Mi'kmaq have had a critical hand in this process.

During the 1950s and 1960s, development of natural resources by dominant sectors of Canadian society created confrontations with First Nations, and the result was a sharp increase in arrests of Native peoples who continued to exercise traditional hunting and fishing rights. During the period, two members of the Vancouver Island Nanaimo band, Clifford White and David Bob, were charged with violating the terms of the Game Act (hunting without a license during the off-season) and the case was taken to the

Supreme Court of British Columbia. On the basis of a series of nineteenth-century treaties, which stipulated that Native peoples were "at liberty to hunt over the unoccupied lands, as formerly," the court held that the treaty agreements could not be abrogated by the provincial government. Since the two men had been apprehended with six deer in their possession, the ruling at least tacitly indicated that First Nations peoples had the right also to commercial harvest.

White and Bob (1965) was a crucial decision that laid the foundation for subsequent Aboriginal victories.[50] The victory presented by the case undergirded a succeeding land claims case that was presented before the Supreme Court in 1973. Speaking on behalf of the Nisga'a, Frank Calder demanded that, since no treaty had ever been negotiated between the Nisga'a and the Canadian government, the government acknowledge Nisga'a ownership of their traditional land base in northern British Columbia. The Supreme Court was split, and the deciding vote, based on a technicality, produced a ruling against the Nisga'a. In the immediate wake of the case, however, public support for the Nisga'a was sufficiently strident that Prime Minister Pierre Trudeau and his Indian affairs minister, Jean Chrétien, initiated land claims negotiations with British Columbia and northern First Nations who had never entered into treaty agreements with the government.[51] The *Calder* case inadvertently brought about the first legal recognition of Aboriginal rights in Canada.

These decisions, and others, created a judicial environment beginning in the 1960s within which the Mi'kmaq were able to press Canadian courts into a discourse involving treaties.[52] In 1985, as I mentioned in Chapter 1, the Supreme Court judged in favor of James Simon, a Mi'kmaw of the Shubenacadie band, who had been convicted in a lower Nova Scotia court of hunting in contravention of provincial game and fishing laws. Simon argued that he had the right to hunt on the basis of provisions of the Treaty of 1752. In *R v. Simon* (1985), the Supreme Court held that the treaty had not been invalidated by subsequent government acts and that Simon was protected by the rights it specified as well as by section 35 of the Canadian Constitution:

> 35. (1) The existing aboriginal and treaty rights of the aboriginal peoples of Canada are hereby recognized and affirmed.
> (2) In this Act, "aboriginal peoples of Canada" includes the Indian, Inuit, and Metis peoples of Canada.

(3) For greater certainty, in subsection (1) "treaty rights" includes rights that now exist by way of land claims agreements or may be so acquired.[53]

R v. Simon was followed by *Denny* (1990), a case in which three Mi'kmaw men were charged with a number of fishing infractions. The men argued in the Nova Scotia Supreme Court that their Aboriginal right to harvest for food superseded provincial regulations, and the court held in their favor.[54] The decision was rendered at the same time that fourteen other Mi'kmaq were facing similar charges of hunting infractions. The province's case against these persons was dropped in the wake of the decision, because the court had clearly ruled on "a presumption of aboriginal rights" in cases of harvesting for food.[55]

A landmark decision followed, that of *R v. Marshall* (1999), to which I referred briefly in the opening chapter. In the mid-1990s, Donald Marshall Jr. was charged with having violated federal fishery regulations by (1) fishing without a license, (2) fishing out of season with an illegal net, and (3) selling fish without a license. The only issue was whether he was protected in these activities by a treaty right that superseded the restrictions of fishery regulations. The trial judge held that he was not thus protected, because the right to fish was implicated in a trade clause within the treaties of 1760 and 1761 and had been nullified when the system of trade ended. The original clause read, in part, "And I do further engage that we will not traffick, barter or Exchange any Commodities in any manner but with such persons or the managers of such Truck houses as shall be appointed or Established by His Majesty's Governor at Lunenbourg or Elsewhere in Nova Scotia or Accadia."[56]

The judge held that along with the dissolution of the system of truck houses (trading posts) also came the termination of any harvesting rights particular to the Mi'kmaw population. The provincial court of appeal upheld the conviction. The case was taken to the Supreme Court of Canada, where the federal government argued that by the Treaty of 1761, the Mi'kmaq had willingly made themselves subject to British—and subsequently Canadian—law and so were bound by federal law. In September 1999, the court held that "the accused treaty rights are limited to securing 'necessaries' (which should be construed in the modern context as equivalent to a moderate livelihood), and do not extend to the open-ended accumulation of wealth. Thus construed, however, they are treaty rights within the meaning of s. 35 of the Constitution Act, 1982."[57]

The present-day conflict over Mi'kmaw harvesting rights is enmeshed in two long-standing and antithetical understandings of the past. Non-Natives have had persistent difficulty understanding why seventeenth-century documents should have any bearing upon contemporary harvesting rights, while Mi'kmaw peoples recognize that the social and economic problems that have plagued their communities to varying degrees over the past two centuries are the direct legacy of generations of disregard for the validity of these formal agreements that defined the parameters of interaction between themselves and non-Native peoples.[58] In a very real sense, the disagreement over Aboriginal and treaty rights has been an epistemological confrontation hinging on the relationship between the Canadian state and First Nations.

It is in the context of this confrontation that I would like to situate the Kluskap myths of the nineteenth and early to mid-twentieth centuries. In spite of their many obvious non-Native embellishments, these myths were not simply fabrications of missionaries, travelers, and scholars; nor should they be regarded as mere cultural artifacts—as Leland said, a part of the "romance of our country," or as a more recent scholar has suggested, stories that have "enriched Canadian culture."[59] These myths were a sacred discourse about originary relationships between the Mi'kmaq, non-Natives, and the land. So long as non-Natives refused to systematically enter into this discourse—in other words, for that period when treaty and Aboriginal rights were barred from the structure of the Canadian judiciary—Kluskap stories affirmed these rights for generations of Mi'kmaw people, assuring them that these rights had a sound (primordial) foundation that was sacred and inviolable.

One such story in particular, recorded by Parsons and published in 1925, seems remarkably appropriate as it speaks of cultural contact as an originary structure, of text (treaties) as part of this structure, and of original sin as a non-Native denial of Mi'kmaw peoples' primordial relationship with landscape:

> He [Christ/God] made a man then, took the earth and made a man. The earth was black, when he got the man to walk, he was dark. This man went hunting all the time. He gave him a bow and arrow, to shoot with. One time he saw this man was getting lonesome. He went and made another man. He got white clay, and this man was a white man. His hair was red.
>
> Man-made-first, God was speaking to him, saying, "That is your own, will be with you all the time." Second-man had a sack, with

papers in it. He was named Hadam. They went along. One day they saw an island in the bay. Man-made-first would go ahead all the time. He said, "We'll go out to the island." Man-made-first walked along on top of the water. He said to the other, "Wherever I put my foot, you put your foot." Second-man said, "Why does he say that? I am just as much of a man as he." So he put his foot down in other places and sank down in the water. Man-made-first said, "You will have to go back now. From the people who come from you, sin will come."[60]

3

THE SAINT ANNE'S DAY MISSION

For a while I thought that my search for Kluskap had reached a plausible
conclusion with the work I had done on the treaties. In fact, I felt pretty certain that there was no reason to continue chasing after him. But a chance
comment from my seventeen-year-old daughter opened my eyes to something that had been staring me in the face for a number of years. And she
upset my sense of closure. We were in Tokyo for a meeting of the International Association for the History of Religions, and following my own presentation on Kluskap and the treaties, we dashed to another venue to hear
Davíd Carrasco and Leonardo Lopez speak about images of Quetzalcoatl
and about sacrifices in the Aztec Great Temple. As we were heading back
down to the street following their presentation—which had been replete
with maps and other images of artifacts, architecture, and landscape—my
daughter said to me, "When you guys talk about actual places and people,
and get away from just ideas, it's really pretty interesting." And before I had
the chance to feel the full sting of that reflection, she added, "Why haven't
you ever talked about Chapel Island and the Saint Anne's Mission?" Chapel
Island, or Potlotek, is located off the coast of Cape Breton Island, and it is
the location of the oldest Catholic mission in Canada.[1] It is also an ancient
burial ground and the site of a monument composed of three large crosses.
I had been told on numerous occasions about the crosses, as well as the
fact that they had a connection with Kluskap. But although I had been to
Potlotek a number of times during the Saint Anne's Mission, I had never

given the crosses much thought. If they were important, I surmised, someone would have shown them to me. Nonetheless, at that moment, walking down a very busy Tokyo boulevard, I told myself that it was perhaps time to ask about them and about their relationship to Saint Anne and Kluskap. I had been invited a few years earlier, after all, to make the connection between the two figures when I had first gone looking for contemporary Kluskap myths. On a number of occasions, when I asked about Kluskap stories, people had spoken instead about Saint Anne. The fact that it had made no sense to me, and that I had essentially ignored it, seemed suddenly to have been a bit foolish.

Over the next couple of years, I would be introduced to an intricate set of relations that exist between the Mi'kmaq; Kluskap; the Peace and Friendship Treaties; and Saint Anne, the grandmother of Jesus. With some friends, and a few of their children and grandchildren, I would walk to the three crosses during the mission. And sitting on the grassy hilltop, I would learn how that monument marked the place of an event that the historian of religion Mircea Eliade would have called a hierophany—a moment in time when the sacred "manifests itself, shows itself, as something wholly different from the profane . . . the manifestation of something of a wholly different order . . . in objects that are an integral part of our natural "profane" world. . . . Every sacred space implies a hierophany, an interruption of the sacred that results in detaching a territory from the surrounding cosmic milieu and making it qualitatively different."[2] The site of the three crosses is the place where it is said by some that Kluskap came to earth seventeen hundred years ago, marking the island as sacred space.[3] In time, I would come to understand a little of the way in which a spatial and ritual structure had been created over centuries at Potlotek that has brought the Peace and Friendship Treaties into this sacred frame—a space that is uniquely Mi'kmaq and distinctly modern.

In exploring this frame, I would be reminded of Walter Mignolo's idea of a "hybrid thinking space"—a space from which it is possible to think in new ways, rather than a space to be merely talked about.[4] In the final chapter of this book, I will explore some theoretical implications of the Saint Anne's Mission as a "thinking space" from which to reconsider the meaning of religion in modernity. Before I do that, however, I want to provide a multidimensional view of this space that has, for generations, provided a context within which the colonial and postcolonial world of Mi'kmaw peoples has been ritually interpreted. This process of interpretation has had many facets, drawing on historical experience, religious symbols, and both oral and written texts. Together these have expressed meanings of both place and language that are at once fully situated within the parameters of what we call modernity and postmodernity and constructively critical of dominant conceptions of both.

Potlotek, as I mentioned earlier, is an island located off the coast of Cape Breton Island, and it is the site of an annual mission to Saint Anne, who is traditionally said to be the patron saint of the Mi'kmaw people.[5] The Mi'kmaq have a long relationship with the Roman Catholic Church, dating back to 1610, when a secular priest named Jessé Fléché baptized Chief Membertou along with twenty members of his family. The relationship with Saint Anne, however, was not introduced for nearly two decades, on the arrival in 1629 of two Jesuits: Barthélémy Vimont and Alexandre de Vieuxpont. Vimont and Vieuxpont arrived in Cape Breton as passengers on a boat commanded by Charles Daniel, who had sailed from France with the intention of bringing provisions to Samuel de Champlain (the French navigator and cartographer considered to be the founder of New France) who was located at Quebec. Daniel's vessel sailed off course in a storm off the Grand Banks of Newfoundland, and the captain was forced to land on Cape Breton Island. There he subsequently constructed the first European fort and chapel—both named for Saint Anne—on the island at Saint Ann's Bay. It was at this time that Vimont and Vieuxpont came into contact with Mi'kmaw peoples and introduced them to the figure of Saint Anne.[6] The two Jesuits had promised their patron, Anne of Austria (the queen mother of France), that they would consecrate the first chapel they built in North America in honor of Sainte Anne d'Apt.[7]

Of all the saints who had emerged from the late medieval period in Europe, Saint Anne was perhaps among the most well suited to transplantation. She had entered into the imagination of Western Europeans predominantly as a result of a store of relics that had been brought back from the Crusades. Her veil, for instance, was said to be housed in Apt Cathedral, and her head had supposedly been brought to the Cathedral at Chartres, where, it was said, "the head of the mother was received with great joy in the church of the daughter."[8] The cult of Saint Anne developed a broad base through the thirteenth and fourteenth centuries, with her feast day of July 26 attaining such popularity that it was granted papal approval in England in 1378 (recognition that was also made in honor of Queen Anne of Bohemia).[9] Anne's rise to prominence has resulted in her being called the "fashionable saint of the period," a figure for whom religious biographies abounded and about whom Martin Luther felt compelled to write in 1537,

"We invoke the help of the saints, creating one saint and deliverer after another. Thus we have made saints of Anna and Joachim [the grandfather of Jesus] not more than thirty years ago."[10] Her cult flourished well into the sixteenth century, but it was officially curtailed when the Council of Trent (1545–63) ruled that the attention paid to the grandmother of Jesus was "misplaced devotion."[11]

Saint Anne was a noticeably malleable figure who melded with pre-Christian symbols in many regions (especially among Celtic peoples) and came to be regarded as the patron saint of birthing mothers, woodworkers, seamstresses, and sailors and was associated with mines, vineyards, and water.[12] In Normandy (the region in which Vimont was born), the feast of Saint Anne was traditionally celebrated over a period of days by ironworkers, carpenters, and lace makers, successively.[13] True to form, Saint Anne seems to have quickly found a place in Mi'kmaw culture, an integration that no doubt also resulted from the high regard with which female elders, and especially grandmothers, were traditionally held. Although the earliest *Jesuit Relations* provide little discussion of the role of seventeenth-century women in Mi'kmaw society beyond issues relating to childbirth, the division of labor, and sexual morality, the broad respect afforded older women can be gleaned from the Récollet Chrétien LeClercq's reference to older women who were regarded as "extraordinary persons, whom they believe to hold converse, to speak familiarly, and to hold communication with the sun, which they have all adored as their divinity."[14]

The association between Saint Anne and the Mi'kmaq was given impetus by Pierre Maillard, a priest who arrived in Cape Breton from the Paris Seminary in 1735 and who spent the next twenty-seven years among the Mi'kmaq. We might note that Maillard was from the town of Chartres, which was an established center of devotion to Saint Anne in France.[15] In his correspondence of the period we find a surprising amount of discussion concerning older Mi'kmaw women and the respect they received from their communities, again pointing to a preexisting cultural framework into which Saint Anne was incorporated.

Maillard wrote of a thanksgiving feast, for instance, which was brought to a close by a speech delivered by the community's oldest woman. In her address, she made note of her accomplishments on behalf of her people: having given birth to "warriors, great hunters, and admirable managers of canoes," having "roused up the spirit of our young men," and having "brought about alliances which there was no room to think could ever be made." These and other achievements, she said, were the products of abilities given to her by the Creator and witnessed by the "river-sides . . . as well as the woods." Furthermore, she had borne the responsibility of torturing and killing prisoners and had done so with a boldness equal to any man's.[16] Maillard would record an episode elsewhere that highlighted not only the part played by old women in dealing with prisoners but also the extreme deference paid these women by their communities. The episode involved an English prisoner who attempted to save himself by pretending both to know Maillard and to be Catholic, and it focused on the ability of only one person—an old woman—to expose the sham. Although Maillard was absent at the time, his servant had made the English prisoner understand that

> as soon as his arms were untied he should cross himself, calling out the holy names of Jesus, Mary and Joseph. . . . The youth followed my servant's instructions almost exactly. However, one thing the Indian omitted to do was to tell the young man to cross himself with his right hand and not his left; and this was his undoing. . . . The Indians . . . could not help noticing these signs of Christianity and even Catholicism. They stayed their hand and looked at each other in perplexity; they knew not what to do for they thought he must be a Christian.
>
> Then one of their old women, Canidies, seeing them transfixed, cried out, "Who has persuaded you to spare this slave? What a small thing it takes to change your mind! If you thought about it for a moment, you would see that instead of being moved to spare his life you would be better to take it immediately, because he is deceiving you. He is not a Catholic! Have him make the sign of the cross a second time. If I can convince you he is deceiving you, hand him over to me. . . ."
>
> "Agreed, grandmother," they replied. The old witch then approached the young mad and said, "Hey! Idiot! *Tchiktoui, n'touèm.* Make the sign of the cross again, *apch k'louchioktogi.*" My man succeeded in interpreting this for the youth, still, however, forgetting to tell him to use his right and not his left hand. So the Englishman crossed himself with his left hand, and thinking he was acting correctly, repeated the action a dozen times.
>
> The old Indian woman turned to the others who were looking on in amazement, and said, "Did you all see which had he used to cross himself? Our priest has told you and me that we must always use the right hand, and not the left to cross ourselves. And what hand did

he use, I ask you? You have all been witnesses. He is therefore not a Catholic, but an Englishmen, *aglachièw wlà*." They replied, "What you say is true: we had not noticed. Take him, grandmother, he is yours."[17]

It was into this context of regard for older women and grandmothers that Maillard was able to successfully interpolate his own devotion to Saint Anne. He directed and personally financed the building of a chapel at Potlotek (the site of an ancient Mi'kmaw burial ground), which he dedicated to the Holy Family and furnished with wooden statues of the Virgin Mary and Saint Anne, the latter of which survived the destruction of the chapel on five occasions.[18] The first occurred when the British torched the chapel and rectory immediately following the French loss of Louisbourg to the English. It occurred, coincidentally, on Saint Anne's Day 1758. The most recent was also by fire, in 1976.[19] The surviving statue of Saint Anne is said to be the same as that which is carried from the chapel in the Saint Anne's Day procession to this day.[20] We should note that the relationship with Saint Anne that was forged during this period has remained a part of the life of the community aside from the annual mission. Contemporary Mi'kmaw pilgrims travel to Sainte Anne de Beaupré, a shrine near Quebec City, during the spring and summer every year.[21] Many spend the fall and winter raising the money to charter buses to make the trip. Although older people tend to make the trip more often than those who are younger, it is not unusual for three or four generations of a family to make it together or for grandparents or parents to travel to the shrine with a sick child in hopes of finding some healing. This is a practice within the Mi'kmaw community that can be documented to at least the mid-nineteenth century. Jerry Lonecloud, for instance, told Clara Dennis that he had begun suffering from seizures when he was a little less than two years old, and his parents "took me in a canoe and went along down the Saint Lawrence River to Saint Anne. I was taken to Saint Anne and cured."[22]

The mission at Potlotek, however, had become a focus for Mi'kmaw Catholicism in the region at least a century earlier. A census of 1752, for instance, reported that although no one was living on the island, many Mi'kmaq were traveling there to celebrate Easter and Pentecost.[23] By 1842, Indian Commissioner Joseph Howe reported that four hundred Mi'kmaw families from across Nova Scotia, Prince Edward Island, and Newfoundland were converging on the island to celebrate the feast of Saint Anne, and by 1876 Chapel Island (Potlotek) was being recognized by non-Natives as one of the three capitals of the Mi'kmaw nation where annual gatherings were held in summer.[24] The precise date at which the mission became an important annual event is difficult to establish, but it was clearly instituted during the time of Maillard along with a number of critical adaptations by the Catholic Church to the style and contingencies of Mi'kmaw Catholicism. Principle among these modifications was the institution of prayer leaders. For nearly a century after the death of Pierre Maillard, the Mi'kmaq lacked the services of a regular priest (indeed, they were completely without a priest during the six years that followed Maillard's death). When they were without priests they relied on a book of idiographic prayers that Maillard had formulated for their use on the basis of a preliminary system of ideograms that had been recorded by LeClercq a century earlier. The book made it possible for the Mi'kmaw community to conduct Sunday services, as well as baptismal, burial, and marriage ceremonies based on the ideographic texts.[25] This concession to what were clearly demands on the part of the Mi'kmaw community (the local Acadians, after all, were not similarly equipped to carry on a sacramental life in the absence of clergy) has been considered by church historians to have ensured the survival of the Catholic Church in Nova Scotia during the early period of British rule.[26]

The feast of Saint Anne itself appears to have been incorporated into a preexisting framework of summer meetings among the Mi'kmaq that had occurred at least as early as the sixteenth century (likely much earlier). These meetings were convened primarily to conduct business that involved a number of bands—war, treaties, and marriages, for example. According to Pierre Biard's Relation of 1616, it was

> principally in Summer that they pay visits and hold their State Councils; I mean that several Sagamores come together and consult among themselves about peace and war, treaties of friendship and treaties for the common good. It is only these Sagamores who have a voice in the discussion and who make the speeches, unless there be some old and renowned *Autmoins,* who are like their Priests, for they respect them very much and give them a hearing the same as to the Sagamores. . . . Now in these assemblies, if there is some news of importance, as that their neighbors wish to make war upon them, or that they have killed some one, or that they must renew the alliance, etc., then messengers fly from all parts to make up the more general assembly, that they may avail themselves of all the confederates, which they call *Ricmaneu,* who are generally those of the same language.[27]

Similarly, LeClercq wrote in the later part of the seventeenth century of "those large assemblies in the form of councils."[28] These meetings were held at various times between April and August at Potlotek, and the shift to a fixed meeting date of July 26 seems to have been concomitant with the establishment of permanent missions in the eighteenth century.[29] While the Mi'kmaq clearly adapted their own traditional pattern of meeting to the constraints of the Catholic liturgical calendar, the church was equally required to adjust to the needs and desires of the Mi'kmaw community. The large summer gatherings that began to occur around the feast of Saint Anne became the most expedient arena for dispensing the sacraments among the Mi'kmaq, and by the late eighteenth century the church had conceded this by providing a dispensation to the Native community that was highly unusual. Traditionally the church required that all Catholics receive the sacrament of the Eucharist at least once a year, and the time specified for the fulfillment of this obligation was the two-week period between the Sunday before and the Sunday after Easter. This was called the "Easter duty." By special permission in some dioceses, the Easter duty time was extended to encompass fourteen weeks, beginning the first Sunday of Lent and ending the Sunday following Pentecost. The Mi'kmaq, however, were granted what is considered to have been a unique dispensation to fulfill their Easter duty at the time of the annual mission in July.[30] Additionally, the mission became the context for administering up to five of the other sacraments, and by the nineteenth century priests from neighboring parishes were required to attend the mission in order to meet the sacramental demands of the Mi'kmaw community gathered there.[31]

While operating within the framework of the church calendar, the mission nonetheless demonstrated decidedly Mi'kmaw management and, further, retained the overt political function of the earlier summer meetings. Chiefs who were subject to allegations of misconduct, for instance, were held accountable before their entire communities at this time. This was the case with Louis Benjamin Pominout, who had received farming implements from a Protestant philanthropist by the name of Walter Bromley in the early nineteenth century. It appears that his acceptance of the equipment from a Protestant was regarded as a conflict of interest, and Pominout was expected to stand before the assembled community on Saint Anne's Day in 1817 and declare his fidelity to the community and the church. "The potatoes, cows, and other provisions of Bromlet . . . are good," he said, "I have taken them and made use of them, but his religion is worthless, I will

have none of it," said the chief, who then proceeded to make a public pro-
fession of faith that was echoed by his political associates."[32]

The political role of the mission assumed new proportions in the wake
of the Canadian government's Indian Act of 1876, when it became the
arena for conducting prescribed band elections and, on rare occasions, dis-
tributing meager profits relating to land and resource sales.[33] By the end
of the century the mission had become something of an institution even
among non-Natives in the region. Osgood's *Handbook for Travelers in the
Maritime Provinces,* for example, directed tourists to a group of islands a few
miles from Saint Peter's, Cape Breton. "On the largest island is a Catholic chapel where all the Micmacs of Cape Breton gather, on the festival of
Saint Anne, every year, and pass several days in religious ceremonies and
aboriginal games."[34] From the turn of the twentieth century to 1950, the
annual mission drew the gaze of a number of scholars, all of whom complained about a deterioration of the event in terms of its "Indian" content.
The role of Native leaders seemed to be diminishing by the decade, and to
some it seemed that the feast day had become a spectacle for non-Native
observers that differed very little from the celebration in other Catholic parishes.[35] "The scenes at Chapel Island," wrote Clara Dennis in 1942, "are not
as spectacular today as they were in the olden days. The feathers, the war
paint, the Indian baskets are missing. The Indian of today is dressed as is
the white man."[36]

By the 1950s, other non-Native observers bemoaned the fact that traditional "beaded frock coats and brilliant sashes" were no longer evident and
that, rather than wearing traditional caps and skirts, women were dressed
in fashions that were current in the wider society. Men had abandoned
their own traditional clothing too, with many choosing to wear, instead,
Plains-styled feather headdresses. Further, one anthropologist noted the
clergy's prohibition of dancing during the mission at Potlotek in the 1940s,
as well as the peculiar presence of unusually quiet uniformed girls from the
Shubenacadie Residential School.[37] From the perspective of these scholars,
whatever had been distinctly Mi'kmaq about the mission was disappear-
ing. However, although they were undoubtedly aware of changes that were
occurring, these observers may not have known precisely what was going
on around them. During the period, the island continued to be regarded as
"holy land,"[38] and it remained a context for transacting traditional forms of
business, as well as for receiving the sacraments of baptism and marriage.[39]
In addition, traditional dances continued to be performed in defiance of

prohibitions against them. During a mission in the late 1940s, for instance, a number of men assembled to dance the *kojuwa* (to be discussed further, below) while members of the community watched them surreptitiously in spite of their apprehension.

Regardless of the obvious biases of many of these observers, as well as their often overt desire to write about a static, non-adaptive Native culture, it is nonetheless true that by the 1970s and 1980s the annual mission had undergone substantial changes, many of which were a direct result, again, of the residential school system that had been in place for most of the century. As three Mi'kmaw leaders noted later, "Our youth were taken away from their families and forced to attend residential schools, where they were beaten to prevent them from speaking their own languages or practicing their culture. The aim of the residential school system was to wipe out any sense of national identity on the part of youth, and replace it with European values and culture. It did not succeed in completely fulfilling these objectives but it did serve to disorient and demoralize three generations of our people."[40]

By the 1980s, this disorientation and demoralization was noticeable at the mission, reflected in an altered ritual structure as well as noticeable alcohol consumption. On the evening before the feast of Saint Anne in 1990 the community was gathered in the chapel and a young woman asked an elder, Annie Mae Bernard, what the ritual actually meant. The old woman asked for silence in the church and proceeded to address the entire congregation, saying that the ritual had become distorted. Alcohol, she said, had traditionally been strictly prohibited on the island during the mission, and persons who consumed alcohol were generally removed to an adjacent island called the "jail." She also noted that the presence of both men and women in the church at that moment was at odds with a time-honored structure of devotion. The Saturday ceremony involved a washing of the statue of Saint Anne, and traditionally only women and children had been involved in the ritual. The act served a number of purposes. It was done, first, as a symbolic offering of the women and children themselves to the grandmother of Jesus, since these were considered to be the most valuable entities the community possessed. The acts of cleansing and honoring were intended also to be a sacred reminder about how to regard and treat all grandmothers. And finally, the rite affirmed the principle that women had the primary ability and responsibility for engendering sanctity in their community. Once the ritual washing had taken place on Saturday, the men could meet to deliberate on Sunday on behalf of the community. Annie Mae Bernard died shortly afterward, but her message was taken to heart. The Saturday ritual was reconstituted the following July as she had suggested, and alcohol was prohibited from the island for the duration of the mission.[41]

The Sunday ritual has remained consistent, as it continues to be a context for expressing the community's religious and political character. An English mass is celebrated in front of the chapel, following which a procession bears the statue of Saint Anne on a litter a distance of about a quarter mile from the chapel to a rise slightly behind a boulder on which Maillard was said to have preached for the first time at Potlotek. Here the *kji'keptan* (grand captain) addresses the people in Mi'kmaq, before the procession turns and makes its way back to the chapel, circles it once, and then reenters it and returns the statue of Saint Anne to her place inside. During the day, the Sante' Mawio'mi meets to deal with business (disagreements between bands, elections, etc.) as it did in the past.

The mission to Saint Anne has, in recent years, received renewed scholarly attention. In this literature, the mission has been interpreted in terms of being something of a balanced incongruity. "Strikingly apparent during the Sunday religious ceremony," writes Janet Elizabeth Chute, "was a symbolic duality," creating a balance "between the Roman Catholic religious aspect and the exclusively Micmac domain of affairs," a "syncretistic blend of Native religion and Roman Catholicism."[42] Anne-Christine Hornborg has described the Sunday ritual as one in which "Catholic and Mi'kmaq traditions were blended"; and Tord Larson strictly differentiates between Native and non-Native aspects of the mission, as though these exist as discreet, reified components: "Of course, people are fully aware of the Christian origin of some of the traditions which have become part of the Micmac display-kit. However, the hymn-singing, the ideographs, and the Saint Anne festival have become such central foci of the tribal community that the non-Native component is not a cause for concern."[43]

There is something familiar, but also a bit unsettling, about this kind of analysis. Is syncretism really the best way to talk about the mission? I am inclined not to think so, and to shy away from this kind of interpretation because I am uneasy about its tacit assumption that opposing cultures can be reconciled and ultimately synthesized in terms that can be fully apprehended by dominant intellectually defining voices while remaining relatively invisible to the colonized. "Syncretism," writes Davíd Carrasco, is "a lazy category"; it is one that masks the "inexactibility of a contact situation."[44] It is "inexactibility" that is indeed at stake here: I do not believe that the mission is simply an amalgamation of distinct and disparate elements. I suggest, instead, that it is a coherent structure that displays characteristics of what Homi Bhabha has called "interstitial" or "in-between" spaces: those arenas of the colonial and postcolonial eras in which inherited cultural forms (both indigenous and colonial) are not simply rearticulated in new configurations but are the fuel behind entirely new conceptions of reality and power.[45] Interstitial spaces are Bhabha's way of identifying the arenas in which cultural identities are created in an ongoing fashion, where ethnicities, nations, classes, genders, and generations crosscut one another and give rise to innovative forms. The cultural forms that emerge from these spaces point to the facts that preexisting cultures are open to transformation and that all cultures are metamorphic (Bhabha prefers the term *hybrid*) entities that are not simply the sum total of earlier forms. Rather, they are "third spaces" from which unique human productions arise:

> If, as I was saying, the act of cultural translation (both as representation and as reproduction) denies the essentialism of a prior given original or originary culture, then we see that all forms of culture are continually in a process of hybridity. But for me the process of hybridity is not to be able to trace two original moments from which the third emerges, rather hybridity to me is the "third space" which enables other positions to emerge. This third space displaces the histories that constitute it, and sets up new structures of authority, new political initiatives, which are inadequately understood through received wisdom.[46]

For Bhabha, ambivalences, marginalities, and hybridities are products of fluctuating cultural boundaries, and they occur when dominant values overflow into what are regarded as peripheral contexts. The hybrid, then, emerges as a site of excess cultural meaning that cannot be explained with earlier interpretive categories, since it points to a radically new structure of authority, emerging from "forms of life and art that do not have a prior existence within the discreet world of any single culture or language."[47] While this kind of formulation is clearly helpful in describing the novel cultural forms that emerge in interstitial spaces, I remain a little uncomfortable with the term *hybridity*. As I mentioned in the introduction, I choose, rather, to use the idea of metamorphosis, acknowledging at the same time the value of the conceptual frame that underlies Bhabha's terminology. I will say a little more about my problems with the idea of hybridity in Bhabha's work in chapter 4.

To begin to understand the way in which the Saint Anne's Mission functions in this manner, we need to turn our attention to both the spatial arrangement of the island and the community's use of that space. In other words, we need to conceptualize the ritual structure within the broader map of Potlotek, and a critical component of this map is the monument to which I referred at the outset of this chapter: the three crosses. About a mile from the chapel, on top of a hill at the center of the island (and hidden entirely from view) is a striking arrangement of three large crosses. The site where they are located is accessible only by a path through a wooded part of the island. These crosses are not the first to have been erected on this spot. During a period in the 1960s, there was only one cross on the island; but prior to that, there were three, although it is not generally known how long these were there. Writers in the 1920s and 1930s, for instance, wrote about a single cross on the island;[48] but whether there was actually only one cross at that time is difficult to know, since it may be that non-Native observers were simply not invited to the site, which would have been impossible for them to locate on their own.[49] We might note here that no recent scholarship on Potlotek or the mission speaks of the crosses, so it seems safe to assume that a lack of references to the three crosses has not been a reflection of their presence or absence.[50]

In spite of this, we can still see the importance of the symbol of three crosses in a 1934 description of the Saint Anne's Day celebration, in which the procession was said to have moved to Maillard's rock, where there was a convergence of three crosses:

> The chapel bell rings out. The Indians assemble. They form into ranks. The little cannon at the rock booms forth. An aged Indian bearing *the cross* advances. The Chief and the clergy follow. The way is lined with those not taking part in the procession. An air of solemnity is over everyone. Even the children have ceased their play and look on with awe. And now comes the shrine, borne by four Indian men and four young Indian girls. The girls are in white with white veils on their heads. Before them walks a boy strewing the way with rose leaves. A choir of Indian men comes next, chanting the Magnificat

in Micmac. Other Indian men, women and children, carrying flags bring up the rear of the procession. The chapel bell keeps ringing and at intervals the little cannon booms forth. The rock is reached—the rock on which the Abbé stood and preached nearly two hundred years ago. *A cross* has been cut on the surface and *an iron cross* set on its top.[51] (My italics)

It is impossible to know whether the monument of the three crosses existed at that time, in addition to this triune symbolism in the procession. Nevertheless, documented material traces the tradition of three crosses at Potlotek to at least the turn of the nineteenth century, when the missionary Vincent de Paul recorded the following in his memoir: "I was obliged to leave and had not time to erect fourteen large crosses which I had intended to place in the middle of the island to serve as a Calvary. They, themselves, made three crosses, probably by this time they have set them up."[52]

For many today, the site is an *axis mundi,* a sacred point that Mircea Eliade would have described as opening a "road to the world of the gods":[53] it is said to be the place where Kluskap came to earth twenty-one generations ago, bringing with him a prophesy known as the "Gift of the Three Crosses." While the prophesy of the Three Crosses has been principally retained in oral form within the community, it has been written down recently. In all likelihood, this is the only instance where this has occurred.

> It was a long time ago when my people were facing complete annihilation; for a long severe drought, covering years, had devastated my people's way of life. The conditions were so bad, that the animals were going blind, the woods were continually catching fire being tinder dry, and fires raged out of control, burning everything in their path. The peoples' suffering was great as the rivers dried up, the fish left the shoreline, and the birds left for lack of food and the animals perished.

> There was an elderly, but very righteous couple who prayed continuously for relief and gave everything they had to their friends, so that their suffering would be lessened. This man, it is said, had great power but was so deeply troubled by the plight of his people, that his power had weakened, by the unnatural conditions that persisted. His inability became a source of shame to him, but his wife of many years strengthened him and prayed unceasingly for the Creator to provide comfort to him and the people he wished to serve.

One night a man came to the lady in a vision. The man was unlike any man she had seen before, and presented himself as coming from the Creator. This holy being told the lady that her people will surely suffer certain death and the end unless the people undertook to save themselves. This could only be secured and accomplished by the people accepting the way of the Cross. The lady was told that the Creator loves our people so much, that the gift of the Cross has been provided to serve, protect and honor this love.

The holy being (some say it was Christ)[54] proceeded to instruct the lady on the meaning of the Cross. "The cross represents the three spirits given to each human being. These three spirits are to be discerned in the following way, the first Cross symbolizes "safe journey," meaning that life is a pilgrimage and one's journey through life is primarily spiritual. This spirit was given to humans so that they may speak directly to the Creator, at any time, on any day, occasion, or place. There is no need for ceremony, ritual or intercession, pray only. The second Cross is called "wise council." The meaning of this spirit relates to the soul that is given to each human. When we speak to one another it is our soul that talks to the others' soul. . . . This is called the covenant of love and protection; the promise that the love of the Creator will guide the soul in searching the soul of the people. It will be necessary in the future for all people to live together. . . .

The third Cross is "full provision." The Creator provides sufficient provision for all. . . .

The three spirits given by the Creator unto each human being will guide their way. It has come to be known as "our" way of life's journey; "our" truth found in wise council; and "our" life of full provision. . . . [55]

Although the prophecy of the Three Crosses has been preserved principally as part of an oral tradition, a much earlier version was recorded in 1688 by Jean-Baptiste de Saint-Vallier, second bishop of Quebec, based on a conversation that had transpired with a Mi'kmaw man who was more than a hundred years old. In spite of the obviously derogatory references to Mi'kmaw religion that the bishop felt compelled to include, there is undeniable symmetry between the two versions:

A long time ago . . . our fathers were afflicted by a cruel famine which depopulated the nation. After having in vain invoked the demon through their juggleries, that is to say through their superstitious ceremonies, one of the oldest of them saw in a dream a young man who, in assuring him of their approaching deliverance through the virtue of the Cross, showed him three of these, of which he declared that one should serve them in public calamities, the other in deliberations and councils, and the third in voyages and perils.[56]

Given that by the time de Saint-Vallier published this book the Mi'kmaq had been associated with the Roman Catholic Church for three-quarters of a century, it would be tempting to attribute the presence of the symbol of the cross to the work of Catholic missionaries in the region. There are at least three mitigating factors, however, that weaken this argument. First, Mi'kmaw peoples of the present day possess an oral history that traces the symbol back to the precontact period. Second, LeClercq referred to the Mi'kmaq in the 1670s as "Cross-bearer Indians" who he contended had knowledge of the symbol prior to the incursion of European Christianity. Finally, LeClercq also related a story concerning an old man who said he had witnessed the arrival of the first European ship in the region:

Well, now, you are a Patriarch. You wish that we believe everything that you tell us, but you are not willing to believe that which we tell you. You are not yet forty years old, and for only two have you dwelt with the Indians; and yet you pretend to know our maxims, our traditions, and our customs better than our ancestors who have taught them to us. Do you not see every day the old man Quioudo, who is more than a hundred and twenty years old? He saw the first ship which landed in our country. He has repeated to you often that the Indians of Mizamichis have not received from strangers the use of the Cross, and that his own knowledge of it has been derived through tradition from his fathers, who lived for at least as long a time as he. Accordingly, you can judge whether we received it before the French came to our coasts.[57]

We have no reason to doubt that the old man was telling the truth and that the cross was a religious symbol among the Mi'kmaq that provided a ready link with Catholic missionaries when they arrived in northeastern North America.

The more recent version of the prophesy was written on the basis of stories told by elders over the past couple of decades. Although it had customarily been preserved in oral form, there was concern that it was becoming increasingly unknown among the youngest generation of Mi'kmaq and that it might disappear. This would be a loss, since some hold that it contains a store of knowledge that is both critical for maintaining social cohesion and necessary for confronting current forms of cultural malaise within contemporary Mi'kmaw communities. Within the prophecy itself there are both a diagnosis of, and a prescription for, these cultural problems: they are linked to colonial contact, and their resolution lies in a new vision of community within this context. "A period of time will pass before another people [the British] much more treacherous than the first [the French], will arrive. They will . . . cause war and harm to be visited upon the people. The Creator will intervene to bring peace and friendship to all; only the way of the Cross becomes the seed for the creation of a great new society on earth."

According to the prophesy, British colonial incursions are the root cause of the trauma with which Mi'kmaw communities are now contending; and the "way of the cross" is the divinely sanctioned formula for healing it: recognition of the relationship between human beings and Niskam (the Creator) and, by virtue of this relationship, the necessity for collective service upon which true freedom (full provision) rests.

Aside from this text (as well as that of de Saint-Vallier), there is another site where this ethical framework appears to have been codified: the series of agreements, collectively known as the Peace and Friendship Treaties, that were negotiated by the Mi'kmaq and British between 1726 and 1761. Some believe that the values expressed in the prophesy were embedded in the treaty-making process, that Mi'kmaw delegates shaped the negotiations by making certain that these principles were integrated into the texts of treaties themselves. Through the treaties, non-Natives conceded that the Mi'kmaq had right to live in peace (specifically, to occupy their land and to harvest its resources unmolested):

Commitment to peace and Recognition of Harvesting Rights
From Treaty of 1752

2. That, all transactions during the late War shall on both sides be buried in Oblivion with the Hatchet. And that the said Indians shall have all favour, Friendship and Protection shewn them, from this His Majesty's Government. . . .

4. It is agreed that the said Tribe of Indians shall not be hindered from, but have free liberty of Hunting and Fishing as usual and that if they shall think a Truckhouse needful at the River Chibenaccadie, or any other place of their resort, they shall have the same built and proper Merchandise lodged therein, to be exchanged for what the Indians shall have to dispose of, and that in the meantime the said Indians shall have free liberty to bring for Sale to Halifax, or any other Settlement within this Province, Skins, Feathers, Fowl, Fish, or any other thing they shall have to sell, where they shall have liberty to dispose thereof to the best advantage. . . .

6. That, to Cherish a good harmony and mutual Correspondence between the said Indians and this Government . . . the said Indians shall upon the first day of October Yearly, so long as they shall Continue in Friendship, Receive Presents of Blankets, Tobacco, some Shott.[58]

There is no doubt that the ethical and practical principle of full provision was guaranteed by the text above (and others like it), as was a commitment to wise council—ongoing constructive conversation between the British and the Mi'kmaq. These values are undeniably integral components of the treaties, which, we should note, are generally regarded by Mi'kmaw peoples as sacred documents. As Donald Marshall Sr., Alexander Denny, and Putus Simon Marshall put it, "The spiritual basis of the treaties is crucial to an understanding of their meaning, since it represents an effort to elevate the treaties, and relations among peoples, beyond the vagaries of political opportunism and expediency. They are intended to develop through time to keep pace with events, while still preserving the original intentions and rights of the parties."[59]

The degree to which British signatories were aware that these values were reflected in the texts of the treaties is obviously impossible to know. However, two of these principles were undeniably at the foundation of the Supreme Court of Canada's ruling in *R v. Marshall* (1999), when the court was asked to interpret the treaty of 1760. The court's judgment was that Donald Marshall's appeal should be allowed because it reflected the Crown's desire to "secure peace and friendship" with the Mi'kmaq in the eighteenth century. In a five-to-two decision, the justices of the court held that the lower court had been in error when it chose to base its decision on the text of the treaty alone. The written treaties, of course, were only half the record of the eighteenth-century agreements, the other half having been preserved in wampum (documents made of beads carved from quahog shells that recorded important communal events) that have disappeared. The Supreme Court justices appear to have been fully sensitive to this fact in their holding, noting, for instance, that the lower court's "overly deferential attitude to the treaty document was inconsistent with a proper recognition of the difficulties of proof confronted by aboriginal people." The justices went on to stress the necessity of admitting "extrinsic evidence" into their deliberations. They held, for instance, that

> the trial judge's narrow view of what constituted "the treaty" led to the equally narrow legal conclusion that the Mi'kmaq trading entitlement, such as it was, terminated in the 1780s. It is the common intention of the parties in 1760 to which effect must be given. The trade clause would not have advanced British objectives (peaceful relations with a self-sufficient Mi'kmaq people) or Mi'kmaq objectives (access to European "necessaries" on which they had come to rely) unless the Mi'kmaq were assured at the same time of continuing access, implicitly or explicitly, to a harvest of wildlife to trade. . . .
>
> Nor is it consistent to conclude that the Governor, seeking in good faith to address the trade demands of the Mi'kmaq, accepted the Mi'kmaq suggestion of a trading facility while denying any treaty protection to Mi'kmaq access to the things that were to be traded, even though these things were identified and priced in the treaty negotiations. The trade arrangement must be interpreted in a manner which gives meaning and substance to the oral promises made by the Crown during the treaty negotiations.[60]

R v. Marshall was a dramatic decision based on a recognition of the principles of ongoing communication and full provision with respect to the treaties. The judges held that the provisions of the Treaty of 1760 were embedded also in the negotiations that surrounded it, and in the discernable "intentions" of the negotiating parties: according to the court these were (1) the maintenance of peace (wise council) and (2) the self-sufficiency of the Mi'kmaq (full provision). We can easily imagine the shadow of Kluskap, whom the Mi'kmaw poet Mary Louise Martin has described as a "Peace Warrior and protector of Mi'kmaq territory," having passed over these deliberations.[61]

However, regardless of either the Mi'kmaw understanding of the treaties or the Supreme Court's decision in 1999, peace, friendship, and full provision were not the outcomes of the eighteenth-century agreements. By the turn of the nineteenth century, the Mi'kmaq were struggling to maintain a radically reduced land base, and legal recognition of their rights of occupation and harvesting had become difficult to achieve, a situation that did not even begin to change at all until the later part of the twentieth century. For the Mi'kmaq, however, the sacred character of the treaties has remained a significant aspect of them, made more obvious by their interrelationship with the site of the annual mission to Saint Anne. Not only are the treaties associated by some with the prophecy of the Three Crosses, but the mission itself became the arena for the ritual repetition of these treaties, as well as another peace treaty with the Mohawk nation. Conflict between the Mi'kmaq and Mohawk was long-standing, but a peace treaty had been negotiated sometime, probably, in the first half of the nineteenth century. Lonecloud, for example, claimed it had occurred as late as the 1860s, but Parsons was told in the 1920s that it had occurred around 1825.[62] Whatever the date of its ratification, the treaty spelled the end of centuries of hostilities.[63] As early as the 1530s, for instance, Jacques Cartier (the first European to map the Saint Lawrence) wrote in the journal he kept in the course of his second voyage to North America that a Mohawk chief had spoken to him of a recent war and had shown him the scalps of five Mi'kmaw casualties of the battle. And in 1610 Marc Lescarbot wrote that "there has always been war between these two nations, as there has been between the Souriquois [Mi'kmaq] and Armouchiquois: and sometimes the Iroquois have raised as many as eight thousand men to war against and exterminate all those who live near the great river of Canada."[64] In the following century, the long-established enmity was exploited by the British, who hired Mohawk warriors to assist them in their war with the Mi'kmaq. A memorial, erected in 1938 at Annapolis Royal, commemorated this relationship: "Site of fort built in 1712 by Mohawk Indians under Major Livingston, employed as allies of the British to intimidate the Micmacs."[65] According to a nineteenth-century historian, fears of an impending Mohawk attack in the early part of the century had the Mi'kmaq preparing for a confrontation, and non-Natives mistaking the activity for an imminent Mi'kmaw attack. "Several strange Indians having been among the Micmacs, Sir John Wentworth suspected that mischief was intended, as some of our Indians appeared in *war paint*. He says the Micmac can only bring 200 men to any purpose they may have. Ideas of a French conquest seem to have been spread among this tribe. The

Mohawks, their ancient foes, whose name was still a bugbear, was made the pretext for their preparations for war, in building canoes, &c."[66]

Hostilities between the two nations appear to have ended in the early to mid-nineteenth century, when, according to Chief John Denys (who spoke with Speck in 1914), both nations simply tired of the needless violence and jointly decided to negotiate a permanent peace.[67] Parsons was told that in 1825 a delegation of six Mi'kmaw men traveled to Khanawake, located on the south shore of the Saint Lawrence River, and negotiated a treaty with the Mohawk.[68] Wampum was exchanged, and the Mi'kmaw delegates gave their Mohawk hosts a evergreen tree called the *kewatk,* which is said to live for hundreds of years, and in return they were given a "welcoming song," to be sung whenever they subsequently entered a Mohawk community. In spite of this peace, even a century later some Mi'kmaq were reported as still regarding the Mohawk as a threat. However, by that time a striking wampum belt (twenty feet in length) commemorating the peace was, along with the treaties with the British, already part of the commemoration of Saint Anne's Day.[69]

Missionaries and ethnographers from the late nineteenth century onward recorded a distinct relationship between the meeting of the Sante' Mawio'mi and a particular dance, and in the early part of the twentieth century they added references to the reading of the treaties during the mission. Helen Webster, in her introduction to Silas Rand's *Legends of the Micmacs,* described "the *wigubaltimk* and *neskouwadijik,* the feast and mystic dance of the *sajawachkik,* the Indians of olden times. At the proper time a chief comes out of a camp, sings a singular tune, dances a singular step, and is responded to by a singular grunt from the assembled crowd."[70]

Within a couple of decades, other writers were referring to the same dances, as well as the public reading of the treaties in the context of the Sante' Mawio'mi's meetings during the mission. In most cases, these writers claimed that the dance and reading were performed by chiefs, but this was not accurate. The meeting of the Sante' Mawio'mi was held in the *kjiwikwam* (the wigwam of the grand chief), located halfway between the chapel and Maillard's rock. According to Lonecloud, it involved about forty people and was led by both the grand chief and putus (wampum reader). Those not directly involved in the meeting (especially women) would stand outside and listen to the proceedings. As one woman told Parsons in the early 1920s, "They made agreement. They had long beads, they read them, Montreal [Mohawk] beads, Cape Breton beads. I could never understand that. They are very particular about listening to that but another woman and I stood in the store back of court house camp [camp of the grand chief] last year and we listened."[71] The meeting would begin with the smoking of a stone pipe by the grand chief, putus, and *keptans* (captains).[72] Tradition holds that the ceremonial smoking of the pipe was a ritual act of peace that has been practiced for thousands of years. "They had this pipe then," Lonecloud told Dennis in the 1920s, continuing:

> They refilled and smoked it before the white people came. The bottom of that pipe was filled then. It is refilled every year.
>
> They did not hear the news for 30 years after [Columbus arrived in America]. Then an Indian went on foot and told this among our chiefs. It was foretold that the whites would come and not to molest them.
>
> Pipe was smoked as peace. This is old legend or story told of the pipe.
>
> Smoked at the time of Columbus. Pipe was used for hundreds and thousands of years before that. It is called the pipe of peace for Cape Breton. They went from the mainland of Nova Scotia and smoked it.[73]

The smoking of the pipe was a significant part of the mission Sunday meeting until midway through the twentieth century. During the period, the *neskewit* (the dance to which Webster and others referred)[74] was the responsibility of the putus who would dance immediately after the Sante' Mawio'mi had completed its deliberations. Following the neskewit, all the men would dance the *kojuwa*, an extremely complicated dance done with black ash rattles that resembled a simultaneous two- and three-step. It was in the context of these dances that the putus would read from original parchment copies of the eighteenth-century treaties and would interpret the *lnu'ap'sku* (wampum) of the treaties with both the British and the Mohawk. Speaking of the treaty with the British, Lonecloud said that the men would "talk the English treaty. We got it from the king long ago to keep it and honor it, honor it and serve it and follow it"; and regarding the Mohawk wampum, he said, "No more fight. Made the piece [*sic*] with Mohawk. Wampum beads are the peace treaty and We read every summer. Andrew Alex [putus] reads them. July 26 the feast of Saint Anne."[75] Speck reported that he was told a decade earlier, "At the national reunion of the Micmac on Saint Ann's day the chief calls the council together and the wampum pledges are exhibited accompanied by the speeches and terms of the treaty. This ceremony requires an entire day. The belts are regarded as sacred and a smoking ceremony precedes the wampum recitations."[76]

The difficult and complex kojuwa, performed between the mass and the reading of the treaties, seems somehow emblematic of the tormented and tenuous relationship that existed between the economically and socially marginalized Mi'kmaw community and the texts that were intended to guarantee the peoples' rights of occupation and harvesting. This practice continued until the late 1960s, when the mission, as we have noted, was showing signs of cultural strain. At that time the original treaties, the wampum, and the pipe disappeared and have not been seen since. The office of putus is hereditary and still exists. But since the texts themselves vanished, the tradition of reading from them directly has been discontinued.

The treaties, however, are still an integral part of the ritual. Following mass, the procession moves to an open rise just behind Maillard's rock, which is located between the chapel and the woods that lead up to the site of the three crosses. From here, the *kji'keptan* addresses the people, focusing substantially on two subjects: (1) the survival of the Mi'kmaw language and (2) the treaties. At the conclusion of this and other speeches, the procession returns to the church. At that spot, halfway between the consecrated space of the church and a place of the hierophany, the treaties are ritually situated in a larger sacred order defined by both Saint Anne and the three crosses. Their place "in between" the chapel and the three crosses marks out a temporal and spatial order that is simultaneously fully modern and fully sacred.

During the time of the mission, Potlotek becomes an ambiguous space in which the Mi'kmaw cosmos in all its multifaceted postcolonial intricacy (including saints, prophets, and hierophanies) and colonial texts (the treaties) converge to articulate a specific understanding of the ordering of modern social relationships and of text itself. While non-Natives, after two hundred years of virtual disregard for the validity of the treaties, have uncomfortably relegated the issue of treaty rights to the judicial system, Mi'kmaw peoples have continued to cyclically reaffirm their vitality and their sacrality. From this perspective, we can discern a critical evaluation of the modern period that differs markedly from other contemporary critiques that have, to varying degrees, emerged in relation to postmodernism. The implication of the mission for both the study of religion in modernity and the meaning of modernity/postmodernity itself will be the focus of our final chapter.

4

KNOWING HOW AND WHERE TO BE

My journey from *Alpha* to Potlotek took a number of years, and it led me through various kinds of research, a lot of conversation, and even some hiking. Through the process, I began to detect a vision of modernity that could not be fully situated in more dominant discourses where modernity had seemingly buckled under itself, clearing a space for the languages of both postmodernism and its critiques. This is the context in which I would like to consider the Saint Anne's Mission, since I believe that the mission reflects a meaning of religion and modernity that cannot not be accounted for within many of our established academic discourses.

Until the 1960s, scholars generally held that the Enlightenment had initiated a scientific, political, and economic shift in Western culture that had ensured that modernity would, as a matter of course, become a secular period. From this perspective, one of the fundamental assumptions underlying modernity was the necessity for creating a rupture with what was regarded as the naivety of the pre-modern period; and to this end, the emergence of the binary concept of secular/religious undercut the idea of transcendence in the West. This movement away from an effective meaning of transcendence reached a peak in the later part of the twentieth century with the concept of postmodernity, an idea that sought to avoid certain kinds of conceits that were implicit in Western modernity.[1] If the idea of religion was destabilized by the rationality of the Enlightenment and its expressed goal of fracturing its intellectual relationship with the medieval period, it was ostensibly rendered obsolete by many postmodernists.

Postmodernism is a mode of thought that sees the contemporary world as a place in which cultural diversity and indeterminacy are inherent features. As Manuel Arriaga says, postmodernism is thus conceived of as a "disruptive event" in the history of the West, engendering as it does a deep skepticism in respect to universalizing Enlightenment concepts such as rationality, objectivity, truth, progress, and freedom.[2] Some argue that the rise of technological capitalism and consumerism underlies the emergence of postmodernist thinking, that this phenomenon altered the relationships among classes to such a degree that older distinctions between elite and popular cultures have been muddled.[3] From this perspective, the experiences of "marginalized" people (for example, the working classes, indigenous peoples, and women) have been sites of alternate cultural meanings that have been historically concealed by Enlightenment discourses, meanings that have emerged from the interrelationships that have characterized these sites.[4]

Narrative (or, more specifically, metanarrative) and text are structures that haunt postmodernist thought and discourse. In North America, postmodernism began in departments of literature and cultural studies and then moved into the arts and architecture. It was the publication of Jean-François Lyotard's La condition postmoderne (1979) that signaled the entrance of philosophy into this discourse, and it was Lyotard who turned the phrase that has arguably remained the most famous formulation of the term postmodern that we have. "Simplifying to the extreme," he wrote, "I define postmodern as incredulity toward metanarratives." At issue in this definition were universalizing ideologies that had provided a cultural foundation for the modern West, but had ultimately failed to provide an adequate basis for social cohesion. On this account, their failure has been responsible for the rise of a general perception of the meaninglessness of life in the West.[5]

Jacques Derrida would take up the state of "incredulity" and turn it loose on the concept of text through a technique he called deconstruction. Derrida's work hinged on the assumption that the West had been metaphysically burdened by "logocentrism" in all its guises, including language, reason, and the concept of God. His critique of modernity was thus framed in terms of writing and, particularly, in respect to his concept of différence—the impossibility of any textual element "referring only to itself." All elements of a text, he argued, refer to other elements not obviously present, such that no text can exist that is not in some sense an entailment of other texts. There is, then, no simple presence or absence that can be identified with any certainty. Rather, there are differences, and "traces" that create a train of meaning. Deconstruction provided a constructive critique of the Western philosophical tradition from the perspective of the inherent instability of language.[6]

There is an aspect of deconstruction that would seem to speak to the historical reality of colonial oppression experienced by communities like the Mi'kmaq. After all, as Mark Taylor has pointed out, deconstruction points to exclusionary acts as the foundation of every cultural structure. From this perspective, all such structures are necessarily the products of things that have been "left out," and once created they tend to become enmeshed in further repression. In a manner reminiscent of Freud's idea of the unconsciousness, Derrida argued that the repressive nature of cultural structures can never be fully successful; that is, those things that are left out may recede from view, but they do not vanish. Rather, they stalk—at times destabilize— the repressive structure.[7] Deconstructionist perspectives on text and metanarrative would together appear to offer us a discursive frame within which to speak of the oppression of peoples in modernity. In fact, I think they do. But in the case of communities like the Mi'kmaq, they do not provide a frame within which that community's experience of modernity can find its own expression. In other words, these postmodernist discourses may be well suited to speaking *about* the marginalization of modern peoples, but they are not so appropriate a mechanism for representing the meanings of modernity that are forged within these so-called marginalized spaces. Whether we are speaking of the instability of text or the unreliability of metanarrative, we are bound within these discourses by discursive parameters that preclude the universalizing sacred as an underlying structure of legitimacy. And in the case of the Mi'kmaq, at least, modernity has not only been an oppressive, marginalizing enterprise; it has also been infused with sacrality. In this instance, religion is not an object of incredulity, nor is it even incidental: it is deeply embedded in the modern world in which this community has found itself.

Postmodernism has undoubtedly pointed to some of the fundamental issues at stake in the creation of the West; and in unmasking the imperious nature of the West's universalizing pretensions, it has shed valuable light on the processes of exclusion that have defined modernity. The place of religion in this discourse, however, has been the source of uneasiness for many in the academy, and their reactions to it provide what could be regarded as alternatives for dealing with religion and modernity. I would like to briefly look at a couple of these alternate discourses that have been particularly influential, with a view to considering their potential for speaking of the kinds of religious forms we have been exploring in the previous chapters. Remaining within the sphere of postmodernism proper, I turn first to the work of Mark Taylor, who has typified the desire to retain an efficacious meaning of religion in a postmodern and post-Enlightenment world. In confronting the problem, he has followed two trajectories. The first involves a mining of the philosophical tradition initiated by Hegel through which, Taylor argues, a deeply religious side of the post-Enlightenment era can be detected.

He begins in tracing a religious turn "inward" that was initiated by Martin Luther and that would find full expression in Kierkegaard's claim that an interiorization of religious sensibility ultimately blurred the distinction between faith and practice. It was Hegel, according to Taylor, who gave this dialectical relationship a fully modern meaning, through his conviction that history had become sanctified in modernity, and religion had become historicized: God was embodied in the world. And it was in the modern West, Hegel claimed, that this embodiment has reached a consummate point:

> The *goal,* Absolute Knowledge, or Spirit that knows itself as Spirit, has for its path the recollection of the Spirits as they are in themselves and as they accomplish the organization of their return. Their preservation regarded from the side of their free existence appearing in the form of contingency is history; but regarded from their comprehended organization, it is the science of knowledge in the sphere of appearance; the two together comprehend history; they form the recollection and the Calvary of Absolute Spirit, the actuality, truth, and certainty of his throne, without which he would be lifeless and alone.[8]

Thus Hegel provides Taylor with an entrée into an active meaning of religion in modernity: Hegel's dialectical formulation points to a religious presence that "haunts" the modern period and expresses itself in a variety of cultural arenas:

> While the theological and metaphysical presuppositions of Hegel's philosophical project might seem dated, the complexity of his

dialectical vision enables us to discern religious dimensions of modernity that less-sophisticated interpreters overlook. Even when appearing resolutely secular, 20th-century culture is haunted by religion. From Mondrian's theosophical painting to Le Corbusier's purist architecture, from Kafka's kabalistic parables to Derrida's deconstructive criticism, from Joyce's Eucharistic vision to Madonna's pop music and videos, and from Alexander Graham Bell's telepathic spiritualism to cyber-culture's telematic mysticism, religion often is most effective where it is least obvious. When analysis is historically and critically informed, it becomes clear that the continuing significance of religion for contemporary culture extends far beyond its established institutions and manifest forms.[9]

Taylor concludes that religion has not been eclipsed, even if it appears so to "less sophisticated" observers.

There are issues raised by this argument. It seems puzzling, for instance, to find a postmodernist turning to primarily examples of cultural elites as indicators of religious life in modernity, given the common concern in postmodernist discourse with listening to "the voices which were submerged by the grand narratives."[10] Perhaps aware of this anomaly, Taylor follows the preceding discussion with a turn to sociological arguments that support the view that religion is a dynamic contemporary phenomenon. Bruce Lincoln, he notes, has pointed out the way in which religion has "recently" begun to function as a tool for political mobilization in modernity:

> In recent years, contradictions between nation and state have also manifested themselves in a particularly debilitating fashion. Where this is so, it has proven relatively easy for militant factions of the population to wage aggressive campaigns in which they seek to redefine the principles on which nation and state are constituted and the ways in which they relate to each other. Of the instruments they have used for mobilization, religious discourse and practice have often been among the most effective, just as their appeals to a sense of religious community have been among the most powerful bases for a novel sense of collective identity.[11]

And Samuel Huntington has argued that religion has often represented the interests of reactionary social forces:

Initially, Westernization and modernization are closely linked, with the non-Western society absorbing substantial elements of Western culture and making slow progress toward modernization. As the pace of modernization increases, however, the rate of Westernization declines and indigenous culture goes through a revival. Further modernization then alters the civilization balance of power between the West and the non-Western society, bolsters the power and self-confidence of that society, and strengthens commitment to the indigenous culture.

In the early phases of change, Westernization thus promotes modernization. In the latter phases, modernization promotes de-Westernization and the resurgence of indigenous culture. . . . At the individual level, modernization generates feelings of alienation and anomie as traditional bonds and social relations are broken and this leads to crises of identity to which religion provides an answer.[12]

Unfortunately, neither of these sorts of formulations (neither religion as a haunting presence nor religion as a predominantly reactive social phenomenon) fully do justice to the kind of experience of the sacred that is at the heart of the story in this book. I might note that Alf Hornborg's analysis of the 1990 conflict over Kelly's Mountain incorporated both these views with, what I suggest, are limited results. "Modernity, while subsuming the mainstream of critique it generates, simultaneously pushes countercultural movements toward extremist positions, including the threat of violence. In redefining the framework of environmental debate, the invocation of spirituality represents another, more successful revolt against the language of modernity."[13] However, what we see in the relations between Kluskap, the treaties, Saint Anne, and Potlotek is a situation in which politics is implicated in a form of religious life (rather than the reverse), and, contra Taylor, this religious mode requires no particular "sophistication" to appreciate.

The second (and more influential) trajectory that Taylor has undertaken has been in the work he calls *a/theology*, in which he explores the implications of the notion of the death of God and searches for a way out of the apparently hollow existence signaled by Nietzsche's classic pronouncement.[14] In this work, Nietzsche meets deconstruction, which Taylor regards as a "hermeneutic of the death of God." From Derrida, Taylor adopts the idea that there are no immutable foundational concepts but only those that are inextricably caught up in a matrix of other concepts. Deconstruction thus signals the death of all "absolutes," since it exposes the way in which everything—including death—is relative. Thus, he concludes that "deconstruction and creation are inseparable," making acquiescence to death a necessary part of coming to live life fully. In *Erring: Postmodern A/Theology*, Taylor makes this argument succinctly. By exploring the meanings of four concepts—God, self, history, and book—he tries to demonstrate how the temporal nature of human life precludes the possibility of individuals conceiving of themselves as unrestricted subjects. This, he argues, leads inevitably to the apprehension of the death of God—but not a form of nihilism. Rather, self and God are reconceived as "markings" and "writing," respectively, with a possibility of redemption reclaimed. "When negation is doubled, it yields affirmation. By negating transcendence, the death of God leads to the total presence of Being here and now."[15] Elsewhere he writes, "God is not the ground of being that forms the foundation of all beings but the figure constructed to hide the originary abyss from which everything emerges and to which all returns. . . . [This abyss] is the anticipatory wake of the unfigurable that disfigures every figure as if from within. Far from simply destructive, disfiguring is the condition of the possibility of creative emergence."[16]

Again, in this postmodern account of God, we cannot find a space in which to represent the experience we have been exploring in the preceding chapters. Taylor sees the death of God as a necessary correlate of the revelation that the human is a finite subject. This, however, is not always so. During the colonial period, a greater part of the world's population confronted exploitation, forced relocation, enslavement, annihilation, and various combinations of these kinds of oppression. This has been a period of death—and not merely in metaphysical terms. The colonial experience has been unmistakably one of confrontation with human limitation, yet we know from even a cursory glance at communities that have undergone this experience that it has not signaled the eclipse of the gods or of the sacred. In fact, what is obvious in situations such as the Saint Anne's Mission is the way in which the colonial and postcolonial periods have been catalysts for new and unique religious experiences.

Aside from postmodernists specifically, there are other scholars who have attempted to confront the problem of religion in the contemporary period by approaching postmodernists' incredulity from a different vantage point. One of the most influential scholars in this regard has been Robert Bellah, who introduced the idea of civil religion in the 1960s. In the years since then, the work of many scholars of religion, theologians, philosophers, historians, and other social scientists has been informed by Bellah's sociological method that is tempered by a regard for the authenticity of religious life. "Since religious symbolism and religious experience are inherent in the structure of human existence," writes Bellah, "all reductionism must be abandoned."[17]

Together, Bellah and scholars influenced by his work have sought not so much to refute postmodern doubts as to circumvent them. "But postmodernist nihilism is not the only realistic response to the dilemmas of modernity. . . . We present exemplars of a third way, an intellectual vision that offers an alternative to positivism and post-modernism, a vision that attempts realistically to confront the dilemmas of modernity but offers hope of transcending them."[18] Although Bellah himself has recognized that the contemporary period is characterized by an awareness of the oppressive force of "dead ideologies," he has not counted religion among these. Rather, he calls into question the post-Enlightenment belief that religion is a vestige of a less sophisticated cultural time, one that would eventually be rendered obsolete by scientific rationalism. Thus he has argued that religion is becoming increasingly important in the West, following an extended period of apparent decline.[19] In exploring this issue, he coined the term "symbolic realism," a concept that has held a continued fascination among scholars of religion.

While postmodernists have responded with skepticism as they have confronted the failure of metanarratives involving religion, moral imperatives, rationality, or freedom, Bellah and many who are influenced by his work have argued that a concept like symbolic realism—the idea that religious symbols express realities that are not reducible to social factors—provides an alternative to skepticism. This idea is an attempt to confront head on the postmodernist reflection that truth (along with other concepts like justice) is an inherently unstable cultural creation. However, rather than fostering an attitude of fundamental doubt toward it, symbolic realism takes up the transformative possibility that accompanies this instability of meaning. We can, by this reckoning, change the trajectory of history while we struggle with the meaning of both the symbols we inherit and the larger social context in which we find ourselves. "Symbols drawn from both the religious and ideological past can, if phrased properly, help us move from the past into the future."[20] One might think that this perspective could more readily accommodate the ritual framework of the Saint Anne's Mission than others that are either exclusionary or reductionist. Again, however, it does not extend that far. How the process works is explored in *Meaning and*

Modernity, a collection of essays in which the contributors turn to what they consider to be an older meaning of religion in order to expose its essential role in our seemingly secular time. Echoing Bellah's reflection that "religion is one . . . because man is one,"[21] the editors assert that all humans are part of one species, and thus all share in some common nature, regardless of how incomplete our understanding of that nature is:

> Justice, for example, as an actual practice is found in all human societies and in some primate ones as well. Perhaps only the axial civilizations have discovered the philosophical concept of justice, and they in slightly different though not incompatible forms. If there is a human nature, even though we may know it only tentatively and in part, then it makes sense to speak of a human telos, a human purpose, something "for the sake of which" we live our lives. . . . If we have a nature, then a good form of life that fulfills the potentialities of our nature *is* our telos. And how do we know what is a good form of life? . . . Our lives are always part of a larger whole, a longer story, that points to something higher than human life, and from which ultimately the standards for a good form of life come. This is what all the axial religions and philosophies have called, in one way or another, God. Those who believe that the telos of human life is most fully expressed in the worship of God have the special responsibility of modeling for us a good form of human life. . . .
>
> One way of putting our present situation would be to say that reality—God—is asking us to embark on a transformation of our way of life, a transformation that would restore our organic relationship to each other and to the biosphere, asking us to struggle to see if we can reconcile the conflicts between freedom and equality that are inherent in our kind of society with the requirements of that organic relationship. . . . If the modern efforts to leap into freedom, noble though they may have been, have led to a form of life that is not sustainable, the axial vision is still alive to help us find a new way.[22]

Does this work offer us a discourse about religion within which to situate Kluskap or the Saint Anne's Mission? The claim that religion is an authentic phenomenon that is not reducible to other social factors is something that could serve us well in this instance. Yet there are other issues at stake in an analysis such as this. Here we find scholars advocating a return to an earlier cultural meaning in order to survive the devastating effects of Enlightenment ideologies. They contend that axial traditions have the philosophical background—and thus, the responsibility— to lead in a transformation of our post-Enlightenment era. Yet the underlying assumption that the philosophical foundations of what Bellah has called the "great world cultures"[23] can save the world that these same foundations have to a substantial degree engendered, seems a bit myopic.

Bellah seems to set the stage for this kind of cultural fixation with specific reference to the modern West in *Beyond Belief*, where he writes:

> It is my feeling that religion, instead of becoming increasingly peripheral and vestigial, is again moving into the center of *our* cultural preoccupations. This is happening both for purely intellectual reasons having to do with the reemergence of the religious issue in the sciences of man and for practical historical reasons having to do with the increasing disillusionment of a world built on utilitarianism and science alone. Religion was the traditional mode by which men interpreted their world to themselves. Increasingly modern man has turned to social science for this interpretation. As social science has attempted more and more to grasp the totality of man it has recognized many of the preoccupations of traditional religion. As traditional religion has sought to relate to the contemporary world it has leaned more and more on social scientific contributions to the understanding of man.[24] (My italics)

What he describes here may well represent the experience of elite voices in the West, but it does not do justice to the experiences of communities that have not found themselves recently disillusioned with science and utilitarianism or those that have had little at stake in the definitions of modernity and religion that have emerged from the social sciences. This kind of perspective passes over the possibility that other kinds of contemporary cultural orders might have cultivated and sustained synchronous and efficacious philosophical or religious meanings of modernity. It is, for instance, difficult to ignore the way in which nonaxial civilizations are categorized in the preceding quotation from *Meaning and Modernity* with primate societies in respect of their philosophical understanding of justice. And we might note that Bellah has also elsewhere drawn a distinction between axial and nonaxial traditions in developmental terms. Speaking of the way in which religion is a reflexive cultural narrative, he notes, "Its history is our history, for we are still imbedded in it more deeply than we consciously imagine,

from tribal peoples to the present."[25] The temporal distinction separating
tribal peoples from the present is specious: there are plenty of modern
tribal societies. Moreover, the underlying assumption that the West and its
traditions can save the world seems unmistakably familiar, and it is difficult
for me to see how this assumption differs substantively from the Enlightenment attitudes that are being called into question.

There are alternatives to reaching back to find models for dealing with
the meaning of religion in modernity, and some of these are to be found in
communities of contemporary people who have contended with Enlightenment ideals of rationality, the individual, and freedom as these have worked
themselves out in the context of modern exploitation and oppression. These
communities have been key players in modernity, while having remained
aloof from efforts to assert the cultural primacy of the West and its history.
In other words, there are modern people who are already doing modernity
differently. Given this fact, the turn to axial visions for salvation from the
problems created by axial cultures seems, at the very least, inexpedient.

At this point, having highlighted a few of the issues that arise when we
attempt to speak of a figure like Kluskap or a phenomenon like the Saint
Anne's Mission in some conventional academic languages, I would like to
turn back to the subaltern framework of Homi Bhabha. In Bhabha we have
a partial entrée into a different kind of discourse that might begin to be
commensurate with the religious experiences of contemporary communities that have come into being "otherwise than modernity."[26] As a literary
theorist, Bhabha's point of departure is the way in which the discourses and
practices of colonialism anticipate issues that come to the fore in contemporary literary theory: internal contradiction, ambivalent and indeterminate
meanings, lack of resolution, and the failure of universalizing concepts.[27]

In many respects, Bhabha's language resonates with that of many postmodernists, and so his work is often described as a derivative of postmodernist discourse.[28] He regards the construction of identity, for instance, as a
process of "persistent questioning of the frame, the space of representation,
where the image . . . is confronted with its difference, its Other."[29] Additionally, his understanding of the prefix *post* (which has been attached to terms
like *modern, feminist,* or *colonial*) has an unmistakably postmodernist feel
to it, referring not to temporality but to the epistemological breaking point
of dominant cultural values that have muted the voices of marginalized
peoples. To be "post" in this sense is to turn to the space in which "something begins its presencing."[30] Again, in Bhabha's work we hear words that
are reminiscent of Derrida. Terms like *difference* and *traces* are often linked

to pivotal reflections on the meaning of culture. On the concept of cultural diversity, for instance, he writes, "Cultural diversity is an epistemological object—culture as an object of empirical knowledge—whereas cultural difference is the process of the *enunciation* of culture as 'knowledge*able*,' authoritative, adequate to the construction of systems of cultural identification. If cultural diversity is a category of comparative ethics, aesthetics or ethnology, cultural difference is a process of signification through which statements *of* culture or *on* culture differentiate, discriminate and authorize the production of systems of cultural identification."[31] Diversity, as Bhabha understands it, is a concept that requires a stable and dominant point of cultural departure in relation to which other cultural forms are situated or, at the very least, a matrix of coexisting fixed identities. And within the concept of "difference," Bhabha envisions cultural "positionalities" that are fluid and changeable.[32] Again, in his critique of the idea of cultural constancy we can hear an echo of Derrida. Speaking of dominant efforts to re-create colonized peoples in the cultural image of colonizing forces, Bhabha points to the futility inherent in the repression of cultural forms. He writes, "The trace of what is disavowed is not repressed but repeated as something different—a mutation, a hybrid."[33]

Although there is no doubt that this work sounds a good deal like post-modernist talk, it also takes a different turn. Thus some have said that it is more accurately a "poststructuralist" discourse that is focused less on the logocentrism that concerns postmodernists than with the shifting ground that lies somewhere between modernity and postmodernity, the space where boundaries digress and identities are transformed.[34] Still others contend that his argument against the possibility of cultural purities places an ostensibly postmodern critique within a postcolonial frame.[35] Bhabha himself, we should note, has generally avoided being entirely circumscribed by any of these. Given the enormous impact that his work has had on all facets of cultural studies, the very difficulty that emerges in trying to classify it points to the inadequacy of current academic discourses to account for the impact of both the practices and languages of colonialism on the shape of modernity. My own inclination, however, is to see his work as postcolonial, though I must offer a caveat: as a model for postcolonial discourse, Bhabha's work is undeniably missing something critical with respect to what would could broadly call the "sacred." I will get to this presently. Still, my preference for *postcolonial* in this case is based in part on Bhabha's own description of his work. "My use of poststructuralist theory," he writes, "emerges from this postcolonial contramodernity. I attempt to represent a certain defeat, or even an impossibility, of the 'West' in its authorization of the 'idea' of colonization. Driven by the subaltern history of the margins of modernity—rather than by the failures of logocentrism—I have tried, in some small measure, to revise the known, to rename the postmodern from the position of the postcolonial."[36]

To my mind, Bhabha's work is not strictly postmodern because the conventional language of metanarrative and logocentrism situates postmodern work in an aesthetic frame; whereas the language to which Bhabha turns refers to things tangible and spatially located: hybridities, borders, edges, "spaces in between." His focus is not on a signifying center that has lost faith in its capacity to find absolute truth but on the contact zones of the colonial enterprise where different cultural meanings emerge. These are, for Bhabha, the "other time and different space" where meanings are forged (and can be spoken about) that are not predicated on the dissolution of Western certainty. Ultimately, this is where such a discourse can serve a space like Potlotek, as well as the wider contemporary world in which Mi'kmaw people reside. Mi'kmaw experience of the colonial and postcolonial periods reverberates with the concerns that Bhabha articulates in the introduction to his most recent edition of *The Location of Culture* where he writes, "I do want to make graphic what it means to survive," he writes, "to produce, to labor and to create, within a world-system whose major economic impulses and cultural investments are pointed in a direction away from you, your country, or your people. Such neglect can be a deeply negating experience, oppressive and exclusionary, and it spurs you to resist the polarities of power and prejudice, to reach beyond and behind the invidious narratives of center and periphery."[37]

Western modernity, as Bhabha has reminded us, came into being in the eighteenth and nineteenth centuries, and the emergence of its discourses concerning the nature of the state, science, culture, and the individual were concomitant with the "visible history of the West as a despotic power."[38] Thus, the colonial experience has been as constitutive of modernity as the universalizing ideas of the Enlightenment. Yet the post-Enlightenment era, as Bhiku Parekh has aptly put it, has been "claustrophobic" in the sense that its universalizing concepts (which have been imposed on much of the world's population) have assumed a normative prerogative that has trivialized and sought to marginalize other cultural meanings. Concurring with Parekh, Bhabha suggests that one of the basic problems of the modern period is the presence of these other forms of cultural knowledge that the West has deemed "archaic" in spite of their contemporaneity.[39] It is this knowledge that exposes some of the more dubious assumptions of Western modernity, and it pervades spaces like the mission at Potlotek.

While this form of postcolonial discourse provides a better academic context within which to situate the mission, it is not, as I mentioned earlier, entirely satisfactory. First, as much as I welcome the use of descriptives such as "spaces in between," other key terms that Bhabha employs may well lock us into conceptual frames in which the West remains normative. *Borders* and *edges,* for example, spatially situate sites of cultural metamorphosis at the margins of the modern world. While coercive power structures have undoubtedly functioned in terms of centers and peripheries, the production of cultural meanings in so-called peripheral zones has not. The term *hybridity* strikes me also as problematic, insofar as it seems to point to stable precursory cultural forms. In this sense, it is a little reminiscent of the idea of syncretism in that it implies a kind of cultural synthesis that can be reduced to its constituent parts and understood in relation to other more normative cultural forms. Second, Bhabha is reluctant to deal with issues relating to language and transcendence "beyond and behind" conventional narratives, and this leaves us empty handed when looking for a way to deal with the unmistakable connection between language and religion in the "other time and space" of Potlotek:

> Too often it is the slippage of signification that is celebrated in the articulation of difference, at the expense of this disturbing process of the overpowering of content by the signifier. The erasure of content in the invisible but insistent structure of linguistic difference does not lead us to some general, formal acknowledgment of the function of the sign. The ill-fitting robe of language alienates content in the sense that it deprives it of an immediate access to a stable or holistic reference "outside" itself. It suggests that social significations are themselves being constituted in the very act of enunciation, thereby undermining the division of social meaning into an inside and an outside.[40]

We are reminded here of Derrida's classic formulation "Il n'y a pas dehors le texte" (There is no thing outside the text), an assumption that serves postcolonial studies well in terms of focusing our attention on the creative power of contact zones and the inherent limitations of Western modernity. Yet when we enter into these zones and pay attention to what is happening within them, there is no denying that religion is an integral component of the experiences, practices, and discourses they generate. In these contexts, religious life defies the postmodern contention that "there is no thing outside the text": the religious modes that emerge in these spaces reveal profound cultural resources that do indeed point to a "stable or holistic" reference point both inside and beyond the immediate temporal and spatial frame within which culture is located. In these situations there are radically new "structures of authority"[41] that are articulated in religious language.

The Saint Anne's Mission at Potlotek is a space in which excess meanings are generated, meanings that point to the reciprocal processes underlying the emergence of modern collective identities. Here we see formulations of culture that expose the essentially metamorphic character of postcolonial communities. But there is something more: the unmistakable presence of a defining structure under which the human enterprise is legitimated. In terms of the West, we hear echoes here of older conceptions of human meaning, but this is a structure that is expressed firmly in the context of modernity. At Potlotek, we are in the presence of fully modern people for whom God is not dead. Charles Long has reminded us that "the language of Western cultural creativity is not the complete language of humankind during this period"; and among the other languages that have defined the post-Enlightenment world is the language of the sacred. "The matter of God is what is being experienced. This may be an old god (but all old gods are new gods). The expression of this god cannot be in the old theological languages. This god has evoked a new beat, a new rhythm, a new movement. It is a god that must be commensurate with both the agony of oppression and the freedom of all persons."[42] At Potlotek during the Saint Anne's Mission, both the metanarratives of the Enlightenment and the violence of the colonial period are subsumed within a community's narrative about its own fundamental meaning in the modern world. Implicit in the ritual is a commentary on the modern West that is different from those I have briefly considered here.

Within many of these dominant discourses, we have been confronted with a skepticism about the religious relationship between language, text, and truth based on what could be regarded as a contradictory assumption that human relationships with language and power in modernity have been universally structured. Walter Mignolo, in his *The Darker Side of Renaissance,* has confronted the limitations of the postmodernist view (with specific reference to Derrida) through an examination of alternate forms of alphabets and writing. I would suggest that a ritual space like that of the Saint Anne's Mission bears on this problem—as well as those of reductionism and Western normativity—in an equally constructive fashion, through its ritual ingestion of modern texts by an alternate sphere of authority.

Reflecting a concern with the relationship between language and the exercise of power, many critiques of modernity have rejected the possibility of a transcendent meaning of language. For the Mi'kmaq, however, the problem of the relationship between language and power is a very much older one. For this community the issue of language and constraint came to the fore concomitantly with the advent of modernity, but the problem has not been about a need to retreat from a transcendent meaning of language. Rather, it has been an issue of locating a signifying structure within which the constraining power of language can be affirmed. For the Mi'kmaq from the late eighteenth century onward, it was the colonizing powers' loss of faith in both the truth of their own language and the capacity of text to express such truth that was at the root of much of the oppression they experienced. Long before postmodernists hailed the end of the possibility of universal claims to truth in text, the Mi'kmaq experienced a dominant culture that had already realized the liberty to act with impunity with regard to the integrity of its own language—in this case, the Peace and Friendship Treaties—and the license this afforded them with respect to practice (for example, appropriation of land, denial of Aboriginal rights). On the eve of Mi'kmaw peoples' forced alienation from land and resources, Nova Scotia's lieutenant-governor Jonathan Belcher spoke eloquently on the British values that buttressed the treaty that had just been renewed. "I meet you now as His Majesty's graciously honoured servant in government and in his royal name to receive at this pillar, your public vows of obedience to build a covenant of peace with you, as upon the immovable rock of sincerity and truth, to free you from the chains of bondage, and to place you in the wide and fruitful field of English liberty."[43]

English liberty was not something that Mi'kmaw peoples would ultimately be permitted to enjoy. And this was because, in a sense, colonials were well on their way to becoming postmodern even as they were becoming modern. In other words, along with the Enlightenment's decentering of God, there came a certain liberation from the constraints of an absolute logos underpinning language and its relationship to practice in the colonial context. It was the restrictive nature of language that was precisely at issue in this situation. The problem was not, however, about the inherent inadequacy of language for representing truth; rather, it concerned the proper sign under which language becomes authoritative. The Mi'kmaw understanding of the treaties is one in which text is regarded as an agent of truth on the basis of its relationship with tradition, sacred symbols, modern myths, and a redefined form of Catholicism. "Tradition," in this context, is not simply a static body of archaic knowledge but a vibrant resource of tested cultural wisdom. A prophesy like the Three Crosses, for example, is just such a resource; and it underscores Ashis Nandy's reflection that "ordinary people make their choices, not because they are prudes who are ill-informed, superstitious, and irrational, but because they make their choices on the basis of traditions that are a cumulation of wisdom and experience acquired over generations and centuries. . . . We have to respect it not because it has a continuity, but because it's like a language tinged with the wisdom of generations, and because often what we offer in exchange are much less thoughtful, much less carefully or cautiously selected alternatives."[44]

So far as the Saint Anne's Mission is concerned, at least, postmodernist discourse might well be an example of such a precipitous alternative. Of course postmodernism, as a critique of modernity, has obviously been the subject of further reflection and critique, much of which has revolved around the assumption that postmodernity is not a particular period in Western history, but a continuing and unsettling part of that entire history. In this sense, it is considered by some to be anachronistic.[45] Terry Eagleton has taken postmodernism to task on just this issue, and his critique provides a good backdrop for my concluding thoughts. Eagleton has suggested that postmodernism does not refer to an "historical stage"; rather, it signals the undoing of historical narratives that function on the basis of developmental principles. The truth of postmodernism, he argues, was inherent in modernity before it was intellectually conceived, since it is simply the recognition of the fictive pretenses of Western modernity. So far, so good. But Eagleton also makes a claim that is rather staggering: "If History as modernity conceives of it is just an illusion, then some postmodernist claims were surely true all along, even though it might be difficult to say *who* exactly they were true *for* [my italics]. There never was any Progress or Dialectic or World Spirit in the first place; this is not the way the world is, or ever was. But postmodern theory is shy of such phrases as 'the way the world is.'"[46] Needless to say, I would suggest that these claims were true *for* the Mi'kmaq and *for* countless others who have been forced to undergo Western modernity.

The Mi'kmaw reflection on modernity that we have explored here could well be more trenchant than those of postmodernism and some of its variations and critiques. It exists not in a denial of the possibility of universal truth that is discernable in text—itself little more than an extension of the Enlightenment project—but in a critique of the desanctification of language itself and the forms of human practice that coincide with this desanctification.[47] For a somewhat poignant illustration of the issues that are at stake here, we might consider Justice Patterson's holding in Grand Chief Gabriel Sylliboy's appeal of his 1928 conviction. As I noted earlier, the conviction was upheld, but it is the judge's remarks in the holding that are worth revisiting here:

> At the trial there was no discussion as to whether the so called treaty was really a treaty or not. Counsel for the defendant, whose closely reasoned brief I cannot too highly commend, did not touch this point. Apparently they are content to accept the description in the document itself, "Treaty or Articles of Peace," but the prosecution raised the question and I must deal with it. Two considerations are involved. First, did the Indians of Nova Scotia have status to enter into a treaty? And second, did Governor Hopson have authority to enter into one with them? Both questions must I think be answered in the negative.[48]

After ruling that the "so called treaty" was not a treaty, Justice Patterson went on to claim that if it had been, it would have had "all the sacredness of a treaty attached to it."[49] With respect to the desanctification of language with which Mi'kmaw peoples have had to contend, there could be perhaps no more cogent statement than this one.

At this point, I wish to return to the Saint Anne's Day Mission at Potlotek and to consider the way in which it expresses what Davíd Carrasco has called "a metamorphic vision of place," in which "change and transformation are sustained patterns. People change places, the places are transformed by hierophanies, and the humans are momentarily and ultimately changed."[50] These sorts of transformations abound at Potlotek. Here, for instance, the grandmother of Jesus has been transformed into the grandmother of the Mi'kmaw people—a figure, like all grandmothers, who is to be trusted and loved unreservedly. The poet Rita Joe wrote of her, "She is the grandmother of Niskam. . . . Our kijinu' [grandmother] in the sky."[51] Unlike other Catholic saints, Saint Anne has been reconceived as a significant figure in and of herself. She is not simply a mediator. By virtue of her position as a grandmother, she embodies a kind of human love that most closely resembles that of the Creator, Niskam. It is a grandmother's profound love that links human beings with their creator, and Saint Anne is the grandmother par excellence. In the transformation of Saint Anne into the grandmother of all Mi'kmaq, there is also an implied relationship between Kluskap and Christ. Most storytellers have stressed that when Kluskap appeared in the world "he brought a woman with him whom he ever addressed as . . . Grandmother."[52] Thus the primordial presence of the Grandmother has traditionally been implicated in the meaning of not only Christ but Kluskap, too—and through him, the Mi'kmaw people. In a related way, the possibility that Kluskap and Christ are the same figure has often been suggested. In the context of speaking about Kluskap's departure, for instance, Jerry Lonecloud told Dennis in the 1920s that "we never knew Christ was crucified until they told us."[53]

Returning to Potlotek, we can see that the island has been repeatedly sanctified: as a burial ground, a site for prophecy, and a center for devotion to Saint Anne. The chapel—originally constructed in honor of the Holy Family—underwent its own transformation in 1999, when it was rededicated to Kateri Tekakwitha, an Algonquin-Mohawk woman who was the first Native nun in Canada and who was canonized in 2012.[54] The alter in the chapel houses relics of both Saint Anne (who could be said to be the first saint in the Catholic pantheon) and Kateri (who is regarded as the first indigenous saint in Canada). On July 26, the procession that bears the statue of Saint Anne moves from the chapel to the rock, and back to the chapel, a succession of motions that is enacted in the shadow of the three crosses—an axis mundi by virtue of the hierophany that is said to have occurred there twenty-one generations ago. At the rise in front of the wooded path leading up to the three crosses, the kji'keptan assumes the position from which Pierre Maillard preached his first sermon and, in the presence of Saint Anne, enacts a ritual incorporation of the eighteenth-century treaties into a cyclical structure of sacrality that is framed by both the hierophany and the tradition of Roman Catholic devotion. Finally, on the island the symbol of the cross has been incorporated into a configuration of sacred power that predates, and has been accommodated to, the colonial period; and it signifies a structure of social order that will follow the period of cultural devastation unleashed by modernity. On Saint Anne's Day, transformed people, places, and symbols come together, and in the space between the chapel and the three crosses, Saint Anne is transported to witness the kji'keptan's affirmation of the treaties. The result is a transcendent meaning of both place and text that is not enmeshed in the asymmetries of power and distrust of universal categories of interpretation at the heart of many contemporary critiques.[55]

The Mi'kmaw understanding of the treaties permits these texts to be fully situated within the modern period that produced them, while being possessed of a sacred character that ensures that they represent something true and binding with respect to practice. Practically speaking, this has helped to ensure that the issue of treaty rights has remained alive among Mi'kmaw peoples, despite a history of disregard for them within dominant sectors of Canadian society. From the vantage point of scholarly discourses, however, I believe that the Saint Anne's Day Mission at Potlotek also provides a significant critique of the post-Enlightenment period, insofar as it affirms the possibility that language and text can be both modern and subject to external sanctification. Recalling one of the myths of Kluskap's creation after all, we know that when Hadam (second man who was white) was created, it was God who gave him "a sack with papers in it."[56]

EPILOGUE

In one sense, this is where I would like to conclude this book. It is a comfortable place to stop, insofar as I have, I believe, thrown a little light on a religious practice that speaks to some of the limitations that are inherent in our contemporary academic discourses. To stop here, however, would be premature, since I also know that the subject that I have been exploring exceeds the cultural language I have to speak of it. To conclude, therefore, I must at least map out a tacit kind of space I have had to confront in saying anything at all, since it rests beneath the ritual structure at Potlotek, my own journey there, and this book. In the concluding chapter of *Alpha*, Charles Long raised two issues that are implicated in this space: (1) myth as a tool for historical research and (2) myth and our modern situation. The first issue has, to a substantial degree, guided the body of this work; but in so doing, it has inevitably brought me face to face with the second. I am a historian of religions, grounded in an academic discipline that, as has often been said, is a child of the Enlightenment. As such, the field shares with other human sciences an elemental ideological tension founded in contradictory impulses that characterized the eighteenth and nineteenth centuries. On the one hand, the emergence of the human sciences was rooted in the idiosyncratic notion that reason was the best means of obtaining knowledge. On the other, the establishment of these sciences was inextricably linked to the violence and unreason of colonialism: the "discovery" of those persons and communities that ultimately underwent the West provided the first inklings and the data for the scientific study of the human species. That contradiction is the burden of this conclusion. Given the difference in origins and traditions that marks my relationship with Mi'kmaw friends, my search for Kluskap was, from the outset, shaped by my desire to pose questions that would mark out some kind of shared space and time from which an authentic conversation could proceed. I felt sure that there had to be a common language about the sacred that could situate my academic quest beyond the contradictory history of violence and inquiry that shapes me as a scholar. What I came to realize, however, is that the central thing we truly share is the colonial background that lurks behind both contemporary Mi'kmaw culture and me as a Western historian of religions. In this sense, perhaps more than in any other, we have common epistemic concerns. As much as I would like it to be otherwise, my search for Kluskap did nothing to elude or neutralize the fact of modern colonial domination. It simply brought it home to me in a new way: for a historian of religions, as for Mi'kmaw peoples, there is nowhere else to go.

I may have come full circle, as I turn back at this point to my introduction to this book, and qualify my suggestion that the mission at Potlotek expresses a critique of modernity. While this suggestion is true, it is also false insofar as it is significant only from my perspective as a member of the modern academy. I have, after all, discerned in this ritual structure a rejoinder to some contemporary academic discourses about modernity and religion that I find less than satisfactory. That said, I also recognize that in and of itself, the sacred framework enacted at Potlotek is not about critique. It is actually at once much more and much less than that, in the sense that it is perhaps an even more penetrating reflection on modernity, and it is to a great degree prereflective. When all is said and done, this is perhaps what has been most difficult for me to grasp as a Western academic. At the mission, Mi'kmaw peoples are not interested in entering into an argument about the meaning and fate of a particular vision of the modern world. In fact, the whole event points to a very different human mode that, while modern, is not defined by being for or against the world as it has been conceived of by dominant voices and actors.

I approach this more thorny issue from the perspective of the concept of a "world," and in this respect, I am influenced by the French sociologist Augustin Berque. Berque defined a world as no more that a particular style of speaking, thinking, feeling, and acting within a landscape. The earth, he wrote, is a world's "*hupokeimenon*: the basis of this predicate being that is as other human worlds are. Thus each world is the unique predicate of a universal subject: nature."[1] For Berque, a world, unlike nature, does not have a universal meaning. All worlds "suppose the biosphere, which supposes the planet, while the reverse is not true: it is a tendency which cannot be reversed because it has a history, that of the contingent emergence of life out of matter and of language and thought out of life."[2] Of course, we know that the modern world has been shaped from its inception by what we call the West, an idea of the world that pervaded the modern effort to supplant the worlds of indigenous peoples across the planet. And in many respects, contemporary academic discourses about modernity have fallen into the same mode of operation. In our drive to repudiate what we now regard as our earlier confusion over the value of Enlightenment universals, for example, we often implicitly assume that our rejection of these universals now provides us with a total meaning of modernity. Berque puts this rather nicely when he writes, "Thus modernity is impregnated with the aporia by which the West, while reducing the Earth to its own world, that is, universalizing it to make it *the* contemporary World, has itself come to recognize its uniqueness, and even to exoticize itself in the eyes of its own social sciences."[3]

In many of our discourses about the contemporary world, metanarratives are alive and well. We remain, for example, somewhat bound to a notion of time that is essentially Hegelian in character. When we speak of the end of metanarratives (or the end of the book, or the subject, or God, for that matter), we simply fall back into a teleological mode in the very act of announcing the end. Moreover, our recent efforts aimed at reforming our self-oriented gaze carry with them an expectation that we can atone for past mistakes and, more critically, that these efforts matter to those who underwent the expansion of our self-orientation. At a profound level, however, they do not. Dominant languages and practices have rarely been Western bedfellows in the eyes of indigenous peoples. By and large, those who survived the West do not expect dominant sectors of society to willingly admit the authentic—and autonomous—situation of indigenous peoples, or to actually address the legacies of injustice except under duress. We might remind ourselves here that the government of Canada did not offer compensation to survivors of residential schools until Nora Bernard and others filed a class action lawsuit, and it took another two years after the settlement of the suit for Canada's prime minister, Stephen Harper, to formally apologize to the generations of Aboriginal peoples who lost their childhoods to these institutions.[4] Essentially, our efforts at reflexive cultural critique may simply be the efforts of one modern tradition trying to come to terms with its own consciousness of the world, and to preserve it as much as is possible in the face of its own mounting discomfort. As Fredric Jameson put it, these efforts may ultimately be no more than the West "theorizing its own condition of possibility."[5]

It is for this reason that, while I have been critical here of dominant academic discourses, I have not offered an alternative. In fact, this is something that I have consciously avoided in writing this book. This text is a product of years of friendships, and in many ways I admit that it may not be an easily categorized piece of work. In my writing style and mode, I have tried very hard to express the curious kind of academic relationship that underlies it. For me, this has meant confronting the reality that I represent a culture of oppression while resisting the urge to rectify this legacy of pain beyond confronting the inadequacy of dominant discourses that deal with the cultures of colonialism and conquest, discourses that do not seem to work. My goal has been simply to mine those inadequacies. In this I have been guided by Claude Lévi-Strauss's dictum that the only culture we can change is our own.[6] In this case, I have pointed my finger at the culture of academic discourse. I suppose this is as prescriptive as I can get in this context: to suggest that we stop signifying, that it hasn't worked. To extrapolate further and offer a prescription would controvert this position.

While the West may have extended itself into virtually every quarter of the earth, it has not overtaken the worlds inhabited by those who were there before and who have suffered that expansion. One of the central aspects of many of these worlds has been a different ordering of time that, although contemporaneous with Western history and deeply engaged with it, has not been part of it. The human mode expressed at Potlotek is a case in point: it implies a discrete temporal ordering that hinges on the earth as an ontological context from which human and social meanings emerge. For Mi'kmaw peoples, time is not bound by the parameters of Western modernity, despite their having to contend with it.

The prophesy of the Three Crosses, for example, locates the colonial period within a temporal frame that predates the fifteenth century, referring to a time of revelation that occurred seventeen hundred years ago. Colonial incursion into the New World was consequently part of the Mi'kmaw world long before the English or the French had even begun to conceive of themselves as cultural and geopolitical entities. And redemption from the ravages of the colonial enterprise is also possible by virtue of the prophesy, but it is based on a Mi'kmaw vision of a connection with the earth as both home and source of life, and the necessity for reciprocity that can ensure that connection. It has nothing to do with the whims or expediencies of the Canadian state. In fact, there is nothing the Canadian state can do to remedy the situation, short of entering into a Mi'kmaw framework of reciprocity and mutuality—a shift that would be typified by a genuine and comprehensive recognition of land and harvesting rights specified in the treaties. Again, in this context, harvesting rights have a primordial foundation in the world-creating labor of Kluskap; they have, as Charles Long would say, an a priori mythic status that ensures that they are permanent,[7] regardless of the vagaries of Canadian gaming and fishing laws. And the treaties intended to ensure these rights have the imprint of Niskam on them. They are infused with sacrality and hearken again to values and sacred powers that are both ancient and fully present in the contemporary world. There is no telos in this configuration of temporality. Time weaves in and around the life of the community in a way that precludes it. Old deities are new deities—Kluskap is present in the New World. And new ones become old—Saint Anne has become the grandmother of all Mi'kmaw peoples. Colonial documents are infused with Mi'kmaw values whose origins are in primordial time and yet speak directly to the lack of cultural reciprocity characteristic of both the colonial and postcolonial situations.

The Mi'kmaw understanding of the treaties, in particular, reveals a meaning of time and of the earth that rests at the foundation of the modern world they inhabit. In this sense, it is not an issue of being for or against the Enlightenment. Mi'kmaw peoples regard themselves as part of a predicated world in which the earth functions as a prereflective repository of meaning that the West, to a substantial degree, has imagined away. This anomaly has been obvious, for instance, in the environmental and human costs that have been associated with the dumping of wastewater into Boat Harbour, a body of water that is adjacent to the Pictou Landing First Nation in Nova Scotia. With government authorization, a pulp mill began dumping its wastewater into the harbor in 1967. The area has become toxic, fish and shellfish are gone, and the people are sick with skin and respiratory illnesses.[8] In 1993, the government agreed to initiate a process of cleaning the area, but as yet it has not made good on that promise. The Mi'kmaw people of Pictou Landing, and the land itself, are living and suffering through a history determined solely by capital gain. This, of course, is a fundamental problem of modernity, stemming from a culture that has effectively negated a humanly constitutive meaning of the earth. The earth is, in Platonic terms, merely the image of an imperceptible form; in Cartesian dualism, simply extension. However we want to depict it, the bottom line is that the earth lacks ontological meaning in the West; it is there to explore and exploit by human beings whose primary mode of being is driven, as Alfred North Whitehead put it, by the desire "(i) to live, (ii) to live well, and (iii) to live better."[9] Noticeably absent from this scenario is any kind of mitigating force, any structure of authority to remind us that we are not the ones who created the world in seven days.

Western history continues to propel us forward into what can ultimately be only an abyss with respect to the sustainability of our own and other species on the earth. In the meantime, communities like the Mi'kmaq are forced to contend with the destructive space and time of the West while maintaining different temporal and spatial orientations that are embedded in the predication of the earth itself and the necessity for relating the human mode to other modes of "being." This is not an archaic structure. It is a dramatically different way of imagining and inhabiting the modern world. The creative possibilities of history may well have been exhausted as the earth staggers under our disenchantment, but history is not the exhaustive repository of possibilities for the world. In fact, the expansion of the West is deeply implicated in other times and spaces that have been open to us all along, times and spaces where reciprocities define the parameters of human action, where the earth is an ontological precondition of being, where enchantment is still possible—where, in the words of Saint Augustine, we are not our own.[10]

Introduction

1. The term *Mi'kmaw* will be employed throughout this book as an adjective and in reference to a single person. When referring to the entire nation, I will use the term *Mi'kmaq*.

2. Sinclair, "Trickster Reflections," 29.

3. Sullivan, "Tricksters," 9350–51.

4. Kelley, "North American Indian Religions," 6661.

5. Morra, "Preface," xii.

6. Perley, "Tricksters," 9357.

7. See Ricketts, "Tricksters," 9355; Fee, "Trickster Moment," 60; Leggatt, "Quintessential Trickster Poetics," 221; Baker, "Coyote Columbus Café," 221; Lynch, *Native American Mythology*, 44.

8. Fagan, "What's the Trouble with the Trickster?" 5.

9. C. H. Long, *Significations*, 51.

10. Pratt, *Imperial Eyes*, 6.

11. Wach, *Essays in the History of Religions*, 177.

12. Carrasco, *To Change Place*, 33.

13. C. H. Long, *Significations*, 154. Jonathan Z. Smith has similarly noted that the New World "for the first time in Western intellectual history raised the theoretical issue of the 'other' as a project of language and interpretation," in short, a "hermeneutical project." J. Z. Smith, "What Difference a Difference Makes," 20–22.

Chapter 1

1. All citations in this book are taken from the Scholars Press edition (1983).

2. C. H. Long, *Alpha*, 38.

3. Ibid., 65, 146.

4. Leland, *Algonquin Legends*, 50, 59, 65, 106.

5. Rand, *Legends*, 339–40; Leland, *Algonquin Legends*, 15–17.

6. Leland, *Algonquin Legends*, 60–61. The theme of regeneration was common to a number of different myths. William Elder recorded another of these in 1871, in which Kluskap is told by a hunting companion, "'The sky is red again, this evening; we shall have a bitter cold night.' It is now Glooscap's turn to struggle with the cold. So he goes home, and sends Little Marten out for fuel, and they build a great fire. But so excessive is the cold, that, by midnight, it is all out, and the old woman and Little Marten are frozen stiff. Next morning, Glooscap calls out, 'Noogŭmē,' numchâseé!' ('Grandmother, get up!') 'Abistănăooch numchâseé!' ('Marten, Get up!') And up they spring, as well as ever." Elder, "Aborigines," 14.

7. "Souvenir of the Micmac Tercentenary Celebration," 26–27; Leland, *Algonquin Legends*, 66–68, 148, 208, 304.

8. C. H. Long, *Alpha*, 190–92.

9. Nowlan, *Nine Micmac Legends*; R. H. Whitehead, *Stories*; Paul, *We Were Not the Savages*; Joe and Choyce, *Mi'kmaq Anthology*; Joe, *Song of Eskasoni*; Runningwolf and Smith, *On the Trail*.

10. A. Hornborg, "Environmentalism"; A.-C. Hornborg, *Landscape*; "Kluskap as Culture Hero"; *Mi'kmaq Landscapes*; "Readbacks or Tradition?"

11. A. Hornborg, "Environmentalism," 247.

12. Readback is a phenomenon in which informants are said to provide anthropologists with material the informants acquired from other anthropologists. See A.-C. Hornborg, "Readbacks," 9.

13. Canadian Broadcasting Corporation, *Fifth Estate*.

14. A. Hornborg, "Environmentalism," 16.

15. In a recent article, Hornborg makes a break with the Kelly's Mountain fiasco, writing instead about Mi'kmaw cosmology and, in particular, that of the pre-contact period. I find this work equally problematic. Hornborg admits that there are distinct problems associated with the attempt to locate evidence for pre-contact cosmology in colonial texts; nonetheless, she relies exclusively on these texts rather than at least augmenting her research with oral history. In addition, her brief references to Kluskap in this essay are erroneous. She claims, for instance, that from the late nineteenth century onward, Kluskap "increasingly assumed the role of a messiah who would return to his people to deliver them from the hardships inflicted by the colonizers" (314). In point of fact, Silas Rand (whom she credits with being the earliest collector of Mi'kmaw myths, which he was not—an error she makes elsewhere too), refers specifically to this kind of redemptive motif. "The Micmacs expect his return in due time, and look for the end of their oppression and troubles when he comes back." See A.-C. Hornborg, "Visiting the Six Worlds."

16. A.-C. Hornborg, "St Anne's Day," 238.

17. A. Hornborg, "Environmentalism," 263.

18. Higashikawa, "Note on the Kluskap Story-Cycle"; Higashikawa and Kimura, "Kluskap and Mi'kmaq Spiritualism." I am indebted to Tatsuo Murakami, Sophia University (Tokyo), for obtaining copies of these articles for me.

19. Parkhill, *Weaving Ourselves into the Land*; Spence, *Myths of the North American Indians*; Campbell, *Historical Atlas of World Mythology*.

20. R. H. Whitehead, *Stories*, 222.

21. Leland, *Algonquin Legends*, 15, 1–3.

22. Roth, *Acadie*, 40–41. Elder, "Aborigines," 13, likewise wrote, "He stands far and above and distinct from all other possessors of supernatural gifts; and a sort of divinity rather than magic seems the foundation of his power." Sweetser, in *Maritime Provinces*, wrote of the "divine Glooscap," 144; and Helen Webster, in her introduction to Rand's *Legends of the Micmacs*, wrote, "He was, to say the least, almost an object of worship," xliv.

23. Leland, *Algonquin Legends*, iii–vi, 1–2.

24. Elder, "Aborigines," 13; Sweetser, *Maritime Provinces*, 144; Hagar, "Weather and the Seasons," 101–2, 104; Roth, *Acadie*, 41. Arion was a legendary Greek poet who was said to have been saved by a dolphin when he was thrown from a ship by his enemies.

25. Bailey, *Conflict*, 135.

26. R. H. Whitehead, *Stories*, 220.

27. Parsons, "Micmac Folklore," 85.

28. Gordon, "Wilderness Journeys," 457–524. See also Runningwolf and Smith, *On the Trail*, 12–15.

29. Rand, *Legends*, 339.

30. Leland, *Algonquin Legends,* 6–7. Leland acquired additional material on Kluskap's birth from a man named Edward Jock.

31. Runningwolf and Smith, *On the Trail,* 12. A reviewer of this book while it was in manuscript form pointed out to me that some of Runningwolf's stories seem to smack of what A.-C. Hornborg calls "readback," resonating with other traditions of storytelling (e.g., the Arthurian tales that seem to be heard in the stories of Kluskap's departure). This is a good point. I am, however, inclined to think that "readback" in this instance would be no different from other Mi'kmaw, rather than the ethnographer's, stories. While he spent his youth in residential schools and received (along with abuse) a Jesuit education, Runningwolf spent a good deal of his childhood listening to the stories of his grandparents and other relatives, stories that have made their way into this book. If "readback" is a salient issue here, it extends over generations.

32. Speck, "Some Micmac Tales," 59. This tradition can be found in the contemporary writing of the poet Mary Louise Martin, who writes, "Glooscap was the first Mi'kmaq created by the breath of the great spirit creator." Martin, "Mi'kmaq Story," 73.

33. Parsons, "Micmac Folklore," 88. Parsons does not name the man until a little later in the story.

34. Ruth Holmes Whitehead published excerpts from the notebooks as *Tracking Doctor Lonecloud: Showman to Legend Keeper.* Where possible, I have cited from this text, since Whitehead's editorial work is excellent. In instances where it does not include a particular text, or where a change of wording seems potentially significant, I have cited from C. A. Dennis, *Field Notes Books 1, 2,* and *6* directly.

35. C. Dennis, *Cape Breton Over,* 51; C. A. Dennis, *Field Notes Book 2,* 2.

36. Speck also noted that "the Micmacs are Gluskap's children." "Some Micmac Tales," 60.

37. R. H. Whitehead, *Tracking Doctor Lonecloud,* 86.

38. Ibid., 89.

39. Runningwolf and Smith, *On the Trail,* 3–4.

40. Webster, introduction, lxiv.

41. Gordon, "Wilderness Journeys," 522.

42. Leland, *Algonquin Legends,* 282.

43. Sweetser, *Maritime Provinces,* 106.

44. Roth, *Acadie,* 42.

45. See, for instance, Hagar, "Weather and the Seasons," 101.

46. Speck, "Some Micmac Tales," 60.

47. C. A. Dennis, *Field Notes Book 1,* 9.

48. Parsons recorded the same vignette. According to Mrs. Poulet, "She was Bear Woman, and at Grandmother Mountain (*gomijagune'wu*) near Baddeck, she is turned to stone. . . . Here is a stone which predicts storm. It gets wet before a storm." "Micmac Folklore," 86.

49. Runningwolf and Smith, *On the Trail,* 129.

50. Conversation with Cheryl Barttelett at Sydney, Nova Scotia, Canada, July 14, 2003. The University College of Cape Breton is now Cape Breton University.

51. Conversation with Murdena Marshall at Eskasoni, Nova Scotia, Canada, July 8, 2003.

52. Conversation with Albert Marshall at Eskasoni, Nova Scotia, Canada, July 8, 2003.

53. Butler, "Shipping Stalls Process." According to Butler, ships go into Little Narrows, "the epicenter of the MSX outbreak," to get gypsum, and they dump the water to make space for their cargo. Little Narrows flows directly into the Brasdor Lakes.

54. Haskin Shellfish Research Laboratory, "Modeling the Oyster Parasite."

55. Mears, "Oyster Diseases."

56. Pine Tree Legal Assistance, "Class Action Suit."

57. Sylliboy, "Teaching of the Mi'kmaq," 130–31.

58. Ramsay, "Turning the Tide"; Health Canada, "Acting on What We Know." The data for issues relating to Mi'kmaw children in particular were incorporated into the Health Canada report from a study undertaken by the Canadian Institute of Child Health, 2000.

59. Rodenhiser, "Bitter Fight Comes to End"; Tutton, "Funeral Underway."

60. Indian and Northern Affairs Canada, "Long-Term Response." The Mi'kmaq share this insufficiency with the Maliseet community, both of whom also have among the highest levels of "on-reserve social assistance dependency."

61. *Simon v. The Queen.*

62. *R v. Marshall.* The Mi'kmaw attorneys were Douglas Brown, Joe B. Marshall, Jim Michael, and Paul Prosper.

63. C. H. Long, *Alpha*, 217, 219–20, 16.

64. Ibid., 11.

65. Ibid., 72–73, 80.

66. Ibid., 218.

67. Conversation with Albert Marshall at Eskasoni, Nova Scotia, Canada, July 8, 2003.

Chapter 2

1. Speck, "Some Micmac Tales," 59; Fauset, "Folklore," 300; Parsons, "Micmac Folklore," 55.

2. Runningwolf and Smith, *On the Trail*, x.

3. Prins, *Mi'kmaq*, 10.

4. The license was obtained by John Julien, on behalf of his band.

5. Reid, *Myth*, 35.

6. Ibid., 42.

7. Elder, "Aborigines," 13.

8. Rand, *Legends*, 24.

9. Parsons, "Micmac Folklore," 87–88.

10. R. H. Whitehead, *Tracking Doctor Lonecloud*, 142.

11. C. A. Dennis, *Field Notes 1*, 16.

12. Runningwolf and Smith, *On the Trail*, xi. In fact, the earliest record of such a myth is found in Gordon's "Wilderness Journeys in New Brunswick."

13. Leavitt, *Maliseet and Micmac*, 89.

14. Antoine Simon Maillard, for instance, whose very extensive *An Account of the Customs and Manners of the Micmakis and Maricheets* (1758) contains references to various supernatural beings in the Mi'kmaq universe, makes no reference to any figure resembling Kluskap. See also A.-C. Hornborg, *Landscape*, 114. Hornborg notes that B. G. Hoffman suggested that the figure of Papkootparout, mentioned by LeClercq, was the equivalent of Kluskap's twin brother, Malsum, but evidence of this association is not sufficient to establish the case. Hoffman, *Historical Ethnography.*

15. Michelson, "Micmac Tales," 53; R. H. Whitehead, *Tracking Doctor Lonecloud*, 145–53; Fauset, "Folklore," 304–5; Parsons, "Micmac Folklore," 86; Speck, "Some Micmac Tales," 59–60.

16. Sweetser, *Maritime Provinces*, 106; Roth, *Acadie*; Rand, *Legends*, xliv, 42; Parsons, "Micmac Folklore," 86.

17. Elder, "Aborigines," 13; Michelson, "Micmac Tales," 53; Parsons, "Micmac Folklore," 86.

18. Roth, *Acadie*, 42; Rand, *Legends*, xliv; Michelson, "Micmac Tales," 53; Parsons, "Micmac Folklore," 86.

19. C. A. Dennis, *Field Notes 6*; Leland, *Algonquin Legends*, 114.

20. Leland, *Algonquin Legends,* 106.

21. Ibid., 50; Wallis and Wallis, *Micmac Indians,* 329.

22. Runningwolf and Smith, *On the Trail,* 7–8. See also Wallis and Wallis, *Micmac Indians,* 305–6.

23. Hagar, "Weather and the Seasons," 101.

24. Rand, *Legends,* xliv; R. H. Whitehead, *Tracking Doctor Lonecloud,* 87; C. A. Dennis, *Field Notes 1,* 2.

25. Speck, "Some Micmac Tales," 60.

26. Sweetser, *Maritime Provinces,* 106.

27. Rand, *Legends,* 232. See also Hagar, "Weather and the Seasons," 101.

28. Sweetser, *Maritime Provinces,* 106; Rand, *Legends,* 232; Speck, "Some Micmac Tales," 60; Wallis and Wallis, *Micmac Indians,* 337.

29. Wallis and Wallis, *Micmac Indians,* 337.

30. Speck, "Some Micmac Tales," 60–61.

31. Wallis and Wallis, *Micmac Indians,* 333–35. Michelson recorded another story in 1925 that pitted Kluskap against the British navy, with subversive results: "They saw a man-of-war. Gloskap and Amkotpigtu went alongside the warship. They begged for their grandmother a pair of scissors, a knife and fork, some thread, some clothes, and some provisions. The boss of the man-of-war had to give what they asked or they would have destroyed him. When they got wanted [*sic*], they went back home." Michelson, "Micmac Tales," 54.

32. Wicken, *Mi'kmaq Treaties,* 127–28.

33. Ibid., 219–20, 3.

34. Although there were antecedents to the doctrine, it was Pope Alexander VI who codified it for the Atlantic world of the fifteenth century, in a two-part papal bull (an official letter or charter) known as *Inter caetera.* The doctrine of discovery was the legal means by which European states claimed rights of sovereignty, property, and trade in regions allegedly discovered during the age of expansion. The doctrine held that once a "discovery" had been made, indigenous peoples could not claim ownership of their own land but only rights of occupation/use, and no indigenous nation could sell its land to any but the discovering nation. The doctrine has been a critical component of historical relations between Europeans, their descendants, and indigenous peoples.

35. Coates, *Marshall Decision,* 38–42, 80–81.

36. Wicken, *Mi'kmaq Treaties,* 218–20.

37. Coates, *Marshall Decision,* 41–42.

38. Wicken, *Mi'kmaq Treaties,* 6.

39. Reid, *Myth,* 81.

40. Coates, *Marshall Decision,* 45.

41. Ibid., 81–82.

42. Roth, *Acadie,* 54.

43. According to Murdena Marshall, granddaughter of the late grand chief, Gabriel Sylliboy was the first elected grand chief of the Mi'kmaq. He was elected in 1918 and remained in the position until 1961. See Ashawasegai, "Historic Mi'kmaq Recordings."

44. R. H. Whitehead, *The Old Man Told Us,* 329.

45. Nova Scotia County Court of Appeal, *Rex v. Syliboy.*

46. R. H. Whitehead, *Stories,* 221.

47. Ibid.

48. Wallis spent another summer collecting material in the 1950s, but the Ki'kwa'ju cycle dates to 1911. Rand spent his summer visiting various bands and, after 1853, spent the rest of his time at his mission at Hantsport, Nova Scotia. As a Baptist missionary, Rand was not very successful (he managed to convert only one person during his forty years among the Mi'kmaq). He was, however, recognized both in Canada and

internationally for his collection of legends and his dictionary of the Mi'kmaw language. See Fingard, "Rand, Silas Tertius."

49. Knockwood, "From 'Out of the Depths,'" 182.

50. *R v. White and Bob.* Cf. Coates, *Marshall Decision,* 83–84.

51. *Calder et al. v. Attorney-General of British Columbia.* Twenty-seven years later, in 2000, the Nisga'a secured a treaty. See Coates, *Marshall Decision,* 84–85.

52. An example of other decisions is *Guerin.* In the 1970s, a private Vancouver golf club obtained a lease from the Musqueam that was negotiated by the federal government on behalf of the First Nation. The lease clearly favored the Shaughnessy Golf Club, and Chief Daniel Guerin, on behalf of the Musqueam, challenged the Department of Indian Affairs for having failed to adequately inform the Musqueam of details concerning the lease. The case was taken to the Supreme Court of Canada, and in 1985 the court ruled that the Musqueam had indeed been dealt with in bad faith. The federal government was ordered to pay ten million dollars. See Coates, *Marshall Decision,* 86.

53. Government of Canada, Constitution Act, 1982. See Coates, *Marshall Decision,* 87; Bell, "Who Are the Métis People," 352.

54. *R v. Denny et al.*

55. Coates, *Marshall Decision,* 89–90.

56. From Treaty of Peace and Friendship, March 10, 1760, between the Mi'kmaq and Governor Charles Lawrence. Cited in Supreme Court of Canada, *R v. Marshall.*

57. Ibid.

58. On these conflicting interpretations, see Coates, *Marshall Decision,* 21.

59. Leland, *Algonquin Legends,* 3; David, *Mi'kmaq,* 43.

60. Parsons, "Micmac Folklore," 88–89.

Chapter 3

1. Potlotek, or Chapel Island, is located in the Bras d'Or Lakes near the community of Saint Peter's, Nova Scotia.

2. Eliade, *Sacred,* 11, 26.

3. One generation in this framework is equal to the space of time between a grandparent and a grandchild.

4. Mignolo, *Darker Side,* xiii.

5. Johnston, *History,* vol. 1, 19.

6. The Jesuit order arrived at Quebec in 1625. Johnston, *History,* vol. 1, 8–9; Chute, "Ceremony," 51. N. N. Smith, "Christian Holidays," 126.

7. N. N. Smith, "Christian Holidays," 126.

8. Ashley and Sheingorn, introduction, 18.

9. Ashley and Sheingorn, *Interpreting Cultural Symbols,* 21.

10. Ibid., 25, 27.

11. Ibid., 43, 47.

12. Sautman, "Saint Anne," 69–70.

13. Ibid., 80. Vimont was born in 1594 in Lisieux.

14. LeClercq, *New Relation,* 229.

15. Johnston, *History,* vol. 1, 65; Lenhart, *History,* 8.

16. Maillard, *Account,* 16–18.

17. Maillard, "Lettre à Madam de Drucourt," translated in R. H. Whitehead, *The Old Man Told Us,* 116–17.

18. Clarissa Archibald Dennis wrote in her notebooks that Jerry Lonecloud told her, "Moosemeal [Maillard] was here for quite a length of time—for some years—he was well

liked. He established a Quahwiggun on an island i.e. it is marsh, but an island when the water surrounds it." C. A. Dennis, *Field Notes 2*, 9.

19. Johnston, *History*, vol. 1, 70.

20. Johnston, *History*, vol. 1, 66–67; C. Dennis, *Cape Breton Over*, 50; Chute, "Ceremony," 53–54. Maillard spent thirty-six hundred livres, for which the governor at Louisbourg requested the French court to reimburse him in 1757.

21. The present-day basilica at Sainte-Anne-de-Beaupré is located on the site of a church built in 1658 to serve the needs of French colonials. During construction, a miraculous healing of a man named Louis Guimond occurred, the first of what would become a common occurrence. As pilgrims began traveling to the shrine, the church had to be expanded on a number of occasions, and in 1876, construction began on the first basilica. Fire destroyed the building in March 1922; a second was built four years later. Sainte-Anne-de-Beaupré Shrine, "History."

22. R. H. Whitehead, *Tracking Doctor Lonecloud*, 51.

23. Johnston, *History*, vol. 1, 69.

24. Johnston, *History*, 108–9; Sweetser, *Maritime Provinces*, 68. By the 1930s, the event had become a popular one for curious non-Natives. See C. A. Dennis, *Field Notes 2*, 6.

25. Johnston, *History*, vol. 1, 73–74; Chute, "Ceremony," 54; C. Dennis, *Cape Breton Over*, 52; Lenhart, *History*, 22.

26. Johnston, *History*, vol. 1, 65.

27. Pierre Biard's Relation, 1616, in Thwaites, *Jesuit Relations*, 87–89.

28. LeClercq, *New Relation*, 234.

29. Chute, "Ceremony," 52.

30. Johnston, *History*, vol. 2, 8; Chute, "Ceremony," 53–54.

31. Johnston, *History*, vol. 2, 239. According to Lonecloud, in the 1930s two priests were at Potlotek to celebrate Mass each day during the mission, with four being required on Mission Sunday. See C. A. Dennis, *Field Notes 2*, 6.

32. Vincent de Paul, *Memoir*, 17–18; see also Chute, "Ceremony," 56–57.

33. Chute, "Ceremony," 56. The Indian Act was passed by the federal government in an attempt to regularize and amalgamate a series of laws that had been enacted as well as earlier treaty negotiations. By the act, Native peoples were made wards of the state, and Indian status was determined on the basis of marriage (Native women who married non-Native men lost their Indian status, while non-Native women who married Native men became legally defined as Indian), and regulations were established relating to the sale of Native land and resources.

34. Sweetser, *Maritime Provinces*, 147.

35. Chute, "Ceremony," 48.

36. C. Dennis, *Cape Breton Over*, 100.

37. Chute, "Ceremony," 47–48. See also Howard, "St. Anne's Day," 10.

38. Parsons, "Micmac Notes," 460.

39. C. Dennis, *Cape Breton Over*, 53.

40. Marshall, Denny, and Marshall, "Covenant Chain," 89–90.

41. Jerry Lonecloud told Clara Dennis that the "jail" was used for dealing with a number of different kinds of infractions: "We got a little Island at Saint Peter's we call it jail and put man there. No one there for 50 years Andrew Newell was last man jailed Cursed and swearing above. Took guns to shoot above He was there a good spell. If a man swears they get punished doing wrong—put there." C. A. Dennis, *Field Notes 2*, 2.

42. Chute, "Ceremony," 50. For an earlier discussion of the Saint Anne's Day ritual as an example of syncretism, see Howard, "St. Anne's Day."

43. A.-C. Hornborg, "St Anne's Day," 249; Larson, "Negotiating Identity," 116.

44. Carrasco, "Jaguar Christians," 133.

45. Bhabha, *Location of Culture*, 2. Mignolo notes that there are reverberations of Bhabha's concept in the "Brazilian novelist and cultural critic Silviano Santiago's notion of 'the inter-space' (*entre-lugar*) of Latin American literature elaborated in the early seventies; [and Gloria] Anzaldúa's notion of 'borderland.'" Mignolo, *Darker Side*, xvi.

46. Rutherford, "Interview," 211. See also Sathianathan, review of *The Location of Culture*, 940.

47. Bhabha, *Location of Culture*, from the introduction to this edition, xiii. See also Gikandi, "In the Shadow," 210–11.

48. Parsons, "Micmac Notes," 460; C. A. Dennis, *Field Notes 2*, 9.

49. It has been suggested to me that non-Mi'kmaq observers did not know that the three crosses existed because the community did not share their location with them.

50. See, for instance, A.-C. Hornborg, "St Anne's Day."

51. C. Dennis, *Cape Breton Over*, 53–54.

52. Vincent de Paul, *Memoir*, 30–31.

53. Eliade, *Sacred*, 35.

54. The use of Christ and Kluskap to connote the same figure is a common practice that can be discerned as well in nineteenth-century myths.

55. Kevin Christmas, unpublished manuscript. Quoted with gratitude.

56. *Estat present de l'Eglise* cited in LeClercq, *New Relation*, 190.

57. LeClercq, *New Relation*, 191. I have edited Ganong's translation to remove archaic wording (for example, "thou wishest" has been changed to "you wish").

58. Paul, *We Were Not the Savages*, 115–16.

59. Marshall, Denny, and Marshall, "Covenant Chain," 75.

60. Supreme Court of Canada, *R v. Marshall*.

61. Martin, "Mi'kmaq Story," 73.

62. C. A. Dennis, *Field Notes 2*, 4; Parsons, "Micmac Folklore," 93.

63. Traditionally, a number of causes for the conflict have been described. A common one that traces to the mid-nineteenth century attributes it to a dispute involving two young boys, into which their respective Mohawk and Mi'kmaw fathers, and then their entire communities, eventually joined. There was a great deal of bloodshed before the Mohawk were forced to retreat to Kahnawake. See Lanman, *Adventures in the Wilds*, 25–26; and Fauset, "Folklore," 305–7. For another explanation involving the reduction of the Mikmaw nation to two individuals, see Lonecloud in C. A. Dennis, *Field Notes 2*, 7–8.

64. Cartier, *Voyages of Jacques Cartier*, 177–78; Marc Lescarbot, "La Conversion des Savages qui ont esté baptizés en la Nouvelle France, cette année 1610," in Thwaites, *Jesuit Relations*, vol. 1.

65. Wallis and Wallis, *Micmac Indians*, 211.

66. Murdoch, *History of Nova Scotia*, 233.

67. Speck, "Some Micmac Tales," 506–7.

68. Parsons, "Micmac Folklore," 23.

69. Some refer to the welcoming song as "Gwan o de." See Ashawasegai, "Historic Mi'kmaq Recordings." Ashawasegai relates the story of a Scottish folklorist, John Lorne Campbell, who traveled to Nova Scotia in 1937 with the intention of recording Gaelic music and songs among the descendants of Highland Scots. While in Nova Scotia, he had the opportunity to record on his ediphone a number of recitations and songs by Grand Chief Gabriel Sylliboy and another man, Levi Poulette. One of these, listed as "A Song sung after treaty between Mohawks and Micmacs," is referred to as "Gwan o de." However, a drummer from Eskasoni who has great familiarity with traditional songs and chants says that it is called "Eeko" and that the peace with the Mohawk was negotiated prior to the treaties with the British. See also Wallis and Wallis, *Micmac Indians*, 208.

70. Webster, "Manners, Customs, Language," xxxi.

71. Parsons, "Micmac Folklore," 93.

72. C. A. Dennis, *Field Notes 2*, 2, 4.

73. Ibid., 2, 7.

74. See also Parsons, "Micmac Notes," 469–72. Maillard mentioned the same dance in a letter in 1755, calling it the *netchkawet*. See Maillard, *Account*, 13.

75. C. A. Dennis, *Field Notes 2*, 2.

76. Speck, "Some Micmac Tales," 507.

Chapter 4

1. Taylor, *Critical Terms*, 2; Benavides, "Modernity," 190, 200.

2. Arriaga, *Modernist-Postmodernist Quarrel*, 77.

3. See, for instance, the introduction to Eagleton, *Illusions*.

4. Joseph, *Interrogating Culture*, 40–41; Berger, *Portable Postmodernist*, viii–ix; Eagleton, *Illusions*, 7.

5. Lyotard, *Postmodern Condition*, 3; Arriaga, *Modernist-Postmodernist Quarrel*, 71; Hinchman and Hinchman, introduction, xiii.

6. Derrida, *Positions*, 26–27. See also Berger, *Portable Postmodernist*, 35; and E. T. Long, *Twentieth-Century Western Philosophy*, 441.

7. Taylor, "What Derrida Really Meant."

8. From the conclusion of the *Phenomenology of Spirit*, cited by Taylor, *Critical Terms*, 3.

9. Taylor, *Critical Terms*, 4.

10. Joseph, *Interrogating Culture*, 41.

11. Lincoln, "Conflict," 66.

12. Huntington, *Clash of Civilizations*, 74–76; cited in Taylor, *Critical Terms*, 5–6.

13. A. Hornborg, "Environmentalism," 242.

14. See Lowe, "Deconstructionist Manifesto," 324.

15. Taylor, *Erring*; "Reframing Postmodernism," 19. See also Lowe, "Deconstructionist Manifesto," 324; Long, *Twentieth-Century Western Philosophy*, 445; and Michener, *Engaging Deconstructive Theology*, 110–11.

16. Taylor, *After God*, 345.

17. Bellah et al., *Beyond Belief*, 253.

18. Madsen et al., introduction, xi. The book includes essays by the editors, as well as by contributors such as Harvey Cox, theologian Stanley Hauerwas, historian Albert Raboteau, philosopher Charles Taylor, and sociologist Robert Wuthnow. The editors of this book also coauthored *Habits of the Heart* with Robert N. Bellah.

19. Bellah et al., *Beyond Belief*, xx, 237, 246.

20. Bellah et al., "What Holds Us Together?" See also Madsen et al., *Meaning and Modernity*, x–xi.

21. Bellah et al., *Beyond Belief*, 256.

22. Madsen et al., *Meaning and Modernity*, 275–76.

23. Bellah et al., "What Holds Us Together?"

24. Bellah et al., *Beyond Belief*, 246.

25. Bellah and Tipton, *Robert Bellah Reader*, 7.

26. Bhabha, *Location of Culture*, 9.

27. Ibid., 248.

28. See, for instance, Gikandi, "In the Shadow," 141; Ellis, review of *The Location of Culture*, 196–97.

29. Bhabha, *Location of Culture*, 66.

30. Ibid., 1.

31. Ibid., 49–50.

32. Ibid., 101.

33. Ibid., 159.

34. See, for instance, Gikandi, "In the Shadow," 139–40.

35. Kwame Anthony Appiah, for instance, has noted that Bhabha's influence has been substantial in postcolonial studies. See Appiah, "Hybrid Age," 5.

36. Bhabha, *Location of Culture*, 175.

37. Ibid., xi.

38. Rutherford, "Interview," 218.

39. Bhabha, "Identities on Parade," 25–27.

40. Bhabha, *Location of Culture*, 235.

41. Rutherford, "Interview," 211.

42. C. H. Long, *Significations*, 65, 212.

43. "Nova Scotia Governor Jonathan Belcher addressing the Mi'kmaq at Halifax, 1761, at ceremonies renewing the Treaty of 1752," cited in Marshall, Denny, and Marshall, "Covenant Chain," 73.

44. Nandy, *Talking India*, 62–63.

45. Arriaga, *Modernist-Postmodernist Quarrel*, 77.

46. Eagleton, *Illusions*, 30.

47. To borrow the words of one critic, Lloyd Spencer, we could say that postmodernism is, in this sense, "modernism under new management." In a similar vein, Gustavo Benavides describes postmodernism as "the intensification of modernity." See Spencer, "Postmodernism," 161; and Benavides, "Modernity," 200.

48. Nova Scotia County Court of Appeal, *R v. Syliboy* (1928).

49. Ibid.

50. Carrasco, *To Change Place*, 33. See also Carrasco, "Jaguar Christians," 132.

51. Joe, "Saint Ann's Picture."

52. Rand, *Legends*, 232. See also Sweetser, *Maritime Provinces*, 106; Leland, *Algonquin Legends*, 60–61; Parsons, "Micmac Folklore," 86–88; C. A. Dennis, *Field Notes 1*, 4.

53. R. H. Whitehead, *Tracking Doctor Lonecloud*, 94.

54. Kateri was the child of a Mohawk father and Algonquin mother, born in 1656 in upper New York State. She was disfigured and left virtually blind by smallpox at four years old and spent her short life (she died at twenty-four years old) in devotion to the church and acts of self-mortification and mutilation, eventually taking the vows at the Mission of Saint Francis Xavier (at Kahnawake, on the Canadian side of the border) that would make her the first Native Catholic nun in North America.

55. Derrida argued that hegemonies required the construct of a primary logos in order to sustain their power.

56. Parsons, "Micmac Folklore," 89.

Epilogue

1. Berque, "Indigenous Beyond Exoticism," 40.

2. Berque, "Ontological Structure."

3. Berque, "Indigenous Beyond Exoticism," 40.

4. The prime minister delivered the apology in the Canadian House of Commons, June 11, 2008.

5. Jameson was writing here particularly about postmodernism. Jameson, *Postmodernism*, ix.

6. "The society we belong to is the only society we are in a position to transform without any risk of destroying it, since the changes, being introduced by us, are coming from within the society itself." Lévi-Strauss, *Tristes tropiques*, 447.

7. C. H. Long, *Significations*, 33.

8. Kenedy, "Fed-Up Aboriginal Community."

9. A. N. Whitehead, "Function of Reason."

10. "God in some degree forsakes you, in consequence of which you grow proud, that you may know that you are 'not your own,' but are His." Saint Augustine of Hippo, *On Nature and Grace*, chapter 32.

BIBLIOGRAPHY

Appiah, Kwame Anthony. "The Hybrid Age." Review of *The Location of Culture*, by Homi K. Bhabha. *Times Literary Supplement*, May 27, 1994, 5.

Arriaga, Manuel P. *The Modernist-Postmodernist Quarrel on Philosophy and Justice.* Lanham, Md.: Lexington Books, 2006.

Ashawasegai, Jennifer. "Historic Mi'kmaq Recordings Found in St. Francis Xavier Library." *Learning Track.* 2006. http://www.fnti.net/media/amsp/lt/2006/mkmaq recordings.html.

Ashley, Kathleen, and Pamela Sheingorn, eds. *Interpreting Cultural Symbols: Saint Anne in Late Medieval Society.* Athens: University of Georgia Press, 1990.

———. Introduction to *Interpreting Cultural Symbols: Saint Anne in Late Medieval Society,* edited by Kathleen Ashley and Pamela Sheingorn, 1–68. Athens: University of Georgia Press, 1990.

Bailey, Alfred Goldsworthy. *The Conflict of European and Eastern Algonkian Cultures, 1504–1700: A Study in Canadian Civilization.* Toronto: University of Toronto Press, 1969.

Bell, Catherine. "Who Are the Métis People in Section 35(2)?" *Alberta Law Review* 29, no. 2 (1991): 351–81.

Bellah, Robert N., Richard Madsen, William M. Sullivan, Ann Swidler, and Steven M. Tipton. *Beyond Belief: Essays on Religion in a Post-traditional World.* Berkeley: University of California Press, 1991.

———. *Habits of the Heart: Individualism and Commitment in American Life.* Berkeley: University of California Press, 1985.

———. "What Holds Us Together?" *The Immanent Frame: Secularism, Religion, and the Public Sphere* (blog), January 11, 2008. http://blogs.ssrc.org/tif/2008/01/11/what-holds-us-together/.

Bellah, Robert, and Steven M. Tripton. *The Robert Bellah Reader.* Durham: Duke University Press, 2006.

Benavides, Gustavo. "Modernity." In *Critical Terms for Religious Studies,* edited by Mark C. Taylor, 186–204. Chicago: University of Chicago Press, 1998.

Berger, Arthur Asa. *The Portable Postmodernist.* Walnut Creek, Calif.: Alta Mira Press, 2003.

Berque, Augustin. "Indigenous Beyond Exoticism." *Diogenes* 50, no. 4 (2003): 39–48.

———. "The Ontological Structure of Mediance as a Condition of Meaning." Paper presented at the conference "Structure and Meaning in Human Settlements," University of Pennsylvania, Philadelphia, October 19–21, 2000. http://www.design.upenn.edu/arch/news/Human_Settlements/ont.html.

Berry, Philippa, and Andrew Wernick, eds. *Shadow of Spirit: Postmodernism and Religion.* London: Routledge, 1992.

Bhabha, Homi K. "Identities on Parade: A Conversation with Bhiku Parekh." *Marxism Today,* June 1989, 2–5.

————. *The Location of Culture*. New York: Routledge, 2006.

Butler, Mark. "Shipping Stalls Process While Bioinvaders Like Oyster-Killer MSX Pour In." 2002. http://www.ecologyaction.ca/news/103961478511996.html.

Calder v. et al. Attorney-General of British Columbia. [1973] S.C.R. 313, 1973.

Campbell, Joseph. *Historical Atlas of World Mythology*. New York: Perennial Library, 1988.

Canadian Broadcasting Corporation. *The Fifth Estate*. With Linden MacIntyre and Trish Wood. Radio broadcast. December 6, 1994.

Carrasco, David. "Jaguar Christians in the Contact Zone: Concealed Narratives in the Histories of Religions in the Americas." In *Beyond Primitivism: Indigenous Religious Traditions and Modernity*, edited by Jacob K. Olupona, 128–38. New York: Routledge, 2004.

————. *To Change Place: Aztec Ceremonial Landscapes*. Niwot: University Press of Colorado, 1998.

Cartier, Jacques. *The Voyages of Jacques Cartier*. Edited by H. P. Biggar. Ottawa: F. A. Acland, 1924.

Chute, Janet Elizabeth. "Ceremony, Social Revitalization, and Change: Micmac Leadership and the Annual Festival of St. Anne." In *Papers of the Twenty-Third Algonquian Conference,* edited by William Cowan, 45–61. Ottawa: Carleton University, 1992.

Coates, Ken S. *The Marshall Decision and Native Rights*. Montreal: McGill-Queen's University Press, 2000.

Cowan, William, ed. *Papers of the Seventh Algonquian Conference, 1975*. Ottawa: Carleton University, 1976.

————. *Papers of the Twenty-Third Algonquian Conference*. Ottawa: Carleton University, 1992.

David, Stephen A. *Mi'kmaq*. Halifax: Nimbus, 1997.

Dennis, Clara. *Cape Breton Over*. Toronto: Ryerson Press, 1942.

Dennis, Clarissa Archibald. *Field Notes Book 1*. Whitehead/Sable edited manuscript, 1992, Nova Scotia Archives and Records Management, MG1, vol. 2867, no. 1, Clara Dennis Collection, Halifax, Nova Scotia, Canada.

————. *Field Notes Book 2*. Whitehead/Sable edited manuscript, 1992, Nova Scotia Archives and Records Management, MG1, vol. 2867, no. 2, Clara Dennis Collection, Halifax, Nova Scotia, Canada.

————. *Field Notes Book 6*. Whitehead/Sable edited manuscript, 1992, Nova Scotia Archives and Records Management, MG1, vol. 2867, no. 6, Clara Dennis Collection, Halifax, Nova Scotia, Canada.

de Paul, Vincent. *Memoir of Father Vincent de Paul, Religious of la Trappe*. Translated by A. M. Pope. Charlottetown, Canada: John Coombs, 1886.

Derrida, Jacques. *Positions*. Edited by Alan Bass. Chicago: University of Chicago Press, 1982.

Eagleton, Terry. *The Illusions of Postmodernism*. Cambridge, Mass.: Blackwell, 1996.

Elder, William. "The Aborigines of Nova Scotia." *North American Review* 230 (January 1871): 1–30.

Eliade, Mircea. *The Sacred and the Profane: The Nature of Religion*. New York: Harcourt, Brace, 1959.

Ellis, Juniper. Review of *The Location of Culture*, by Homi K. Bhabha. *Philosophy and Literature* 19, no. 1 (1995): 196–97.

Fagan, Kristina. "What's the Trouble with the Trickster?" In *Troubling Tricksters: Revisioning Critical Conversations,* edited by Deanna Reder and Linda M. Morra, 3–20. Waterloo, Ontario: Wilfred Laurier University Press, 2010.

Fauset, Arthur Huff. "Folklore from the Half-Breeds in Nova Scotia." *Journal of American Folk-Lore* 38, no. 148 (1925): 300–315.

Fee, Margery. "The Trickster Moment, Cultural Appropriation, and Liberal Imagination in Canada." In *Troubling Tricksters: Revisioning Critical Conversations,* edited by Deanna Reder and Linda M. Morra, 59–76. Waterloo, Ontario: Wilfred Laurier University Press, 2010.

Fingard, Judith, "Rand, Silas Tertius." *Dictionary of Canadian Biography.* http://www.biographi.ca/EN/ShowBio.asp?BioId=39908.

Gikandi, Simon. "In the Shadow of Hegel: Cultural Theory in an Age of Displacement." *Research in African Literatures* 27, no. 2 (1996): 139–50.

Gordon, Arthur. "Wilderness Journeys in New Brunswick." In *Vacation Tourists and Notes of Travel in 1862–63,* edited by Francis Galton, 457–524. London: Macmillan, 1864.

Government of Canada. Constitution Act, 1982. http://laws.justice.gc.ca/en/const/annex_e.html.

Hagar, Stansbury. "Weather and the Seasons in Micmac Mythology." *Journal of American Folk-Lore* 10, no. 36 (1897): 101–5.

Haskin Shellfish Research Laboratory. "Modeling the Oyster Parasite: MSX." http:/vertigo.hsrl.rutgers.edu/msx.html.

Health Canada. "Acting on What We Know: Preventing Youth Suicide in First Nations." http://www.hc-sc.gc.ca/fnih-spni/pubs/suicide/prev_youth-jeunes/sec.

Higashikawa, Yoichi. "A Note on the Kluskap Story-Cycle: An Introduction to Micmac Story." *Hakodate Eibungaku: Journal of the English Literary Society of Hakodate* 32 (March 31, 1993): 1–12.

Higashikawa, Yoichi, and Masatsuga Kimura. "Kluskap and Mi'kmaq Spiritualism." *Hakodate eibungaku: Journal of the English Literary Society of Hakodate* 32 (March 31, 1993): 13–22.

Hinchman, Lewis P., and Sandra K. Hinchman. Introduction to *Memory, Identity, Community: The Idea of Narrative in the Human Sciences,* edited by Lewis P. Hinchman and Sandra K. Hinchman, xiii–xxxii. Albany: State University of New York Press, 1997.

———. *Memory, Identity, Community: The Idea of Narrative in the Human Sciences.* Albany: State University of New York Press, 1997.

Hoffman, B. G. "The Historical Ethnography of the Micmac of the Sixteenth and Seventeenth Centuries." PhD diss., University of California, 1946.

Hornborg, Alf. "Environmentalism, Ethnicity, and Sacred Places: Reflections on Modernity, Discourse, and Power." *Canadian Review of Sociology and Anthropology* 31, no. 3 (1994): 245–67.

Hornborg, Anne-Christine. "Kluskap as Culture Hero and Global Green Warrior: Different Context for the Canadian Culture Hero." *Acta Americana,* 9, no. 1 (2001): 17–38.

———. *A Landscape of Left-Overs: Changing Conceptions of Place and Environment Among Mi'Kmaq Indians of Eastern Canada.* Lund Studies in History of Religions, 14. Lund, Sweden: Religionshistoriska avdelningen, Lunds universitet, 2001.

———. *Mi'kmaq Landscapes: From Animism to Sacred Ecology.* Aldershot, U.K.: Ashgate, 2008.

———. "Readbacks or Tradition? The Kluskap Stories Among Modern Canadian Mi'kmaq." *European Review of North American Studies* 16 (2002): 9–16.

———. "St Anne's Day—a Time to 'Turn Home' for the Canadian Mi'kmaq Indians." *International Review of Mission* 91, no. 361 (2002): 237–55.

———. "Visiting the Six Worlds: Shamanistic Journeys in Canadian Mi'kmaq Cosmology." *Journal of American Folklore* 119, no. 473 (2006): 312–36.

Howard, James H. "The St. Anne's Day Celebration of the Micmac Indians, 1962." *Museum News* 26 (March/April 1965): 5–13.

Huntington, Samuel. *The Clash of Civilizations and the Remaking of World Order*. New York: Simon and Schuster, 1996.

Indian and Northern Affairs Canada. "Long-Term Response to the Marshall Decision: Overview of Indian and Northern Affairs Strategy." 2004. http://www.ainc-inac .gc.ca/pr/info/ltr_e.html.

Jameson, Fredric. *Postmodernism; or, The Cultural Logic of Late Capitalism*. Durham: Duke University Press, 2001.

Joe, Rita. *Lnu and Indians We're Called*. Charlottetown, Canada: Ragweed, 1991.

———. "Saint Ann's Picture on Deerhide." In *Lnu and Indians We're Called*, 46. Charlottetown, Canada: Ragweed, 1991.

———. *Song of Eskasoni: More Poems of Rita Joe*. Charlottetown, Canada: Ragweed Press, 1988.

Joe, Rita, and Lesley Choyce, eds. *The Mi'kmaq Anthology*. Lawrencetown Beach, Canada: Pottersfield Press, 1997.

Johnston, Angus Anthony. *A History of the Catholic Church in Eastern Nova Scotia*. Vol. 1, 1611–1827. St. Francis Xavier University Press: Antigonish, Canada, 1960.

———. *A History of the Catholic Church in Eastern Nova Scotia*. Vol. 2, 1827–1880. St. Francis Xavier University Press: Antigonish, Canada, 1971.

Joseph, Sarah. *Interrogating Culture: Critical Perspectives on Contemporary Social Theory*. New Delhi: Sage, 1998.

Kelley, Dennis F. "North American Indian Religions: Mythic Themes." In *Encyclopedia of Religion*, edited by Lindsay Jones, 6658–64. 2nd ed. Farmington Hills, Mich.: Macmillan Reference USA, 2004.

Kenedy, Kaley. "Fed-Up Aboriginal Community Demanding Clean Up, Halifax Media Co-Op." May 25, 2010. http://halifax.mediacoop.ca/story/3485.

Knockwood, Isabel. "From 'Out of the Depths.'" In *The Mi'kmaq Anthology*, edited by Rita Joe and Lesley Choyce, 164–94. Lawrencetown Beach, Canada: Pottersfield Press, 1997.

Lanman, Charles. *Adventures in the Wilds of the United States and British American Provinces*. Vol. 2. Philadelphia: John W. Moore, 1856.

Larson, Tord. "Negotiating Identity: The Micmacs of Nova Scotia." In *The Politics of Indianness: Case Studies of Native Ethnopolitics in Canada*, edited by Adrian Tanner, 37–136. St. John's: Institute of Social and Economic Research, Memorial University, 1983.

Leavitt, Robert M. *Maliseet and Micmac: First Nations of the Maritimes*. Fredericton, Canada: New Ireland Press, 1995.

LeClercq, Chrestien. *New Relation of Gaspesia, with the Customs and Religion of the Gaspesian Indians*. Translated by William F. Ganong. Toronto: Champlain Society, 1910.

Leggatt, Judith. "Quintessential Trickster Poetics: Lenore Keeshig-Tobias's 'Trickster Beyond 1992: Our Relationship' (1992) and Annharte Baker's 'Coyote Columbus Café' (1984)." In *Troubling Tricksters: Revisioning Critical Conversations*, edited by Deanna Reder and Linda M. Morra, 221–38. Waterloo: Wilfred Laurier University Press, 2010.

Leland, Charles Godfrey. *The Algonquin Legends of New England or Myths and Folk Lore of the Micmac, Passamaquoddy, and Penobscot Tribes*. Boston: Houghton Mifflin, 1884.

Lenhart, John. *History of the Micmac Ideographic Manual*. Sydney, Canada: Nova Scotia Native Communications Society, 1976. First published 1932.

Lescarbot, Marc. "La conversion des savages qui ont esté baptizés en la Nouvelle France, cette année 1610." In *Jesuit Relations and Allied Documents*, edited by Rueben Gold Thwaites. Vol. 1. Cleveland: Burrows Brothers, 1959: 49–112.

Lévi-Strauss, Claude. *Tristes tropiques*. Translated by John Weightman and Doreen Weightman. New York: Pocket Books, 1977.

Lincoln, Bruce. "Conflict." In *Critical Terms for Religious Studies*, edited by Mark C. Taylor, 55–69. Chicago: University of Chicago Press, 1998.

Long, Charles H. *Alpha: The Myths of Creation*. New York: George Braziller, 1963; New York: Macmillan, 1969. Reprint, Atlanta, Ga.: Scholars Press, 1983.

———. *Significations: Signs, Symbols, and Images in the Interpretation of Religion*. Aurora, Colo.: Davies Group, 1999.

Long, Eugene Thomas. *Twentieth-Century Western Philosophy of Religion, 1900–2000*. Boston: Kluwer Academic, 2003.

Lowe, Walter. "A Deconstructionist Manifesto: Mark C. Taylor's *Erring*." *Journal of Religion* 66, no. 3 (1986): 324–31.

Lynch, Patricia. *Native American Mythology A–Z*. New York: Chelsea House, 2010.

Lyotard, Jean-François. *The Postmodern Condition: A Report on Knowledge*. Minneapolis: University of Minnesota Press, 1984.

Madson, Richard, William M. Sullivan, Ann Swidler, and Steven M. Tipton. Introduction to *Meaning and Modernity: Religion, Polity, and Self*, edited by Richard Madsen, William M. Sullivan, Ann Swidler, and Steven M. Tipton, ix–xvii. Berkeley: University of California Press, 2002.

———, eds. *Meaning and Modernity: Religion, Polity, and Self*. Berkeley: University of California Press, 2002.

Maillard, Antoine Simon. *An Account of the Customs and Manners of the Micmakis and Maricheets*. London: Hooper and Morley, 1758.

Marshall, Donald, Sr., Alexander Denny, and Putus Simon Marshall. "The Covenant Chain." In *Drumbeat: Anger and Renewal in Indian Country*, edited by Boyce Richardson, 71–104. Toronto: Summerhill Press, 1989.

Martin, Mary Louise. "Mi'kmaq Story of Turtle Love." In *The Mi'kmaq Anthology*, edited by Rita Joe and Lesley Choyce, 73–75. Lawrencetown Beach, Canada: Pottersfield Press, 1997.

Mears, Gregory. "Oyster Diseases of the Chesapeake Bay: MSX Facts Sheet," 2003. http://www.vims.edu/env/projects/oysters/msx.html.

Michelson, Truman. "Micmac Tales." *Journal of American Folk-Lore* 38 (1925): 33–54.

Michener, Ronald T. *Engaging Deconstructive Theology*. London: Ashgate, 2007.

Mignolo, Walter. *The Darker Side of the Renaissance: Literacy, Territoriality, and Colonization*. Ann Arbor: University of Michigan Press, 1995.

Morra, Linda. "A Preface: Ruminations About Troubling Tricksters." In *Troubling Tricksters: Revisioning Critical Conversations*, edited by Deanna Reder and Linda M. Morra, xi–xii. Waterloo: Wilfred Laurier University Press, 2010.

Murdoch, Beamish. *A History of Nova Scotia, or Acadie*. Vol. 3. Halifax, Canada: James Barnes, 1867.

Nandy, Ashis. *Talking India: Ashis Nandy in Conversation with Ramin Jahanbegloo*. New Delhi: Oxford University Press, 2006.

Nova Scotia County Court of Appeal. *Rex v. Syliboy, 1928*. Kingston: McGill-Queen's University Press. http://www.apcfnc.ca/court.asp?ID=127&type=Archived.

Nowlan, Alden. *Nine Micmac Legends*. Hantsport, Canada: Lancelot Press, 1983.

Olupona, Jacob K., ed. *Beyond Primitivism: Indigenous Religious Traditions and Modernity*. New York: Routledge, 2004.

Parkhill, Thomas. *Weaving Ourselves into the Land: Charles Godfrey Leland, "Indians," and the Study of Native American Religions*. Albany: State University of New York Press, 1997.

Parsons, Elsie Clews. "Micmac Folklore." *Journal of American Folk-Lore* 38 (1925): 55–133.

————. "Micmac Notes: St. Ann's Mission on Chapel Island, Bras D'Or Lakes, Cape Breton Island." *Journal of American Folklore* 39 (1926): 460–85.

Paul, Daniel N. *We Were Not the Savages: A Micmac Perspective on the Collision of European and Aboriginal Civilization.* Halifax, Canada: Nimbus, 1993.

Perley, Bernard C. "Tricksters: North American Tricksters [Further Considerations]." In *Encyclopedia of Religion,* edited by Lindsay Jones, 9356–57. 2nd ed. Farmington Hills, Mich.: Macmillan Reference USA, 2004.

Pine Tree Legal Assistance. "Class Action Suit Filed by Former Students of the Shubenacadie Indian Residential School." *Wabanaki Legal News,* Summer 1988. http://www.ptla.org/ptlasite/wabanaki/shubenacadie.htm.

Pratt, Mary Louise. *Imperial Eyes: Travel Writing and Transculturation.* New York: Routledge, 1992.

Prins, Harold. *The Mi'kmaq: Resistance, Accommodation, and Cultural Survival.* New York: Holt, Rinehart and Winston, 1996.

Ramsay, Heather. "Turning the Tide on Suicide." *Tyee,* December 5, 2007. http://thetyee.ca/News/2007/12/05/NativeSuicide/.

Rand, Silas Tertius. *Legends of the Micmacs.* New York: Longmans, Green, 1894.

Reder, Deanna, and Linda M. Morra, eds. *Troubling Tricksters: Revisioning Critical Conversations.* Waterloo, Canada: Wilfred Laurier University Press, 2010.

Reid, Jennifer. *Myth, Symbol, and Colonial Encounter: British and Mi'kmaq in Acadia, 1700–1867.* Ottawa: University of Ottawa Press, 1995.

Rex v. Syliboy. [1929] 1 D.L.R. 3.0.7., 50 C.C.C. 389, 1929.

Richardson, Boyce, ed. *Drumbeat: Anger and Renewal in Indian Country.* Toronto: Summerhill Press, 1989.

Ricketts, Mac Linscott. "Tricksters: North American [First Edition]." In *Encyclopedia of Religion,* edited by Lindsay Jones, 9354–56. 2nd ed. Farmington Hills, Mich: Macmillan Reference USA, 2004.

Rodenhiser, David. "Bitter Fight Comes to End." *Daily News,* December 16, 2006. http://nativeamericantherealdeal.tribe.net/thread/d739abd4-3107-44fa-b6f5-0395846 1a77c.

Roth, D. Luther. *Acadie and the Acadians.* Utica, N.Y.: L. C. Childs, 1891.

Runningwolf, Michael B., and Patricia Clark Smith. *On the Trail of Elder Brother: Glous'gap Stories of the Micmac Indians.* New York: Persea Books, 2000.

Rutherford, Jonathan, ed. *Identity: Community, Culture, Difference.* London: Lawrence and Wishart, 1990.

————. "Interview with Homi Bhabha." In *Identity: Community, Culture, Difference,* edited by Jonathan Rutherford, 207–21. London: Lawrence and Wishart, 1990.

R v. Denny et al. [1990] 94 N.S.R. (2d), 1990.

R v. Marshall. [1999] 3 S.C.R. 533, 1999.

R v. White and Bob. [1965] 52 D.L.R. (2d) 481, 1965.

Sainte-Anne-de-Beaupré Shrine. "History." http://www.ssadb.qc.ca/en/histoire.htm.

Sathianathan, Sudarshan. Review of *The Location of Culture,* by Homi K. Bhabha." *Ethnic and Racial Studies* 19, no. 4 (1996): 940–41.

Sautman, Francesca. "Saint Anne in Folk Tradition: Late Medieval France." In *Interpreting Cultural Symbols: Saint Anne in Late Medieval Society,* edited by Kathleen Ashley and Pamela Sheingorn, 69–94. Athens: University of Georgia Press, 1990.

Sim, Stuart, ed. *The Routledge Companion to Postmodernism.* New York: Routledge, 2001.

Simon v. The Queen. [1985] 2 S.C.R. 387, 1985.

Sinclair, Niigonwedom. "Trickster Reflections." In *Troubling Tricksters: Revisioning Critical Conversations,* edited by Deanna Reder and Linda M. Morra, 21–58. Waterloo: Wilfred Laurier University Press, 2010.

Smith, Jonathan Z. "What Difference a Difference Makes." In *"To See Ourselves as Other See Us": Christians, Jews, "Others" in Late Antiquity,* edited by Jacob Neusner and Ernest Frerichs, 3–48. Chico, Calif.: Scholars Press, 1985.

Smith, Nicolas N. "Christian Holidays Important to the Wabanaki." In *Papers of the Seventh Algonqian Conference, 1975,* edited by William Cowan, 115–28. Ottawa: Carleton University, 1976.

Souvenir of the Micmac Tercentenary Celebration, 1618–1910. Restigouche, Canada: Frères Mineurs Capuchins, n.d.

Speck, Frank G. *Beothuk and Micmac.* New York: Museum of the American Indian, Heye Foundation, 1922.

———. "Some Micmac Tales from Cape Breton Island." *Journal of American Folk-Lore* 28 (1915): 59–69.

Spence, Lewis. *The Myths of the North American Indians.* London: G. G. Harrap, 1914.

Spencer, Lloyd. "Postmodernism, Modernity, and the Tradition of Dissent." In *The Routledge Companion to Postmodernism,* edited by Stuart Sim, 125–134. New York: Routledge, 2001.

Sullivan, Lawrence E. "Tricksters: An Overview." In *Encyclopedia of Religion,* edited by Lindsay Jones, 9350–52. 2nd ed. Farmington Hills, Mich.: Macmillan Reference USA, 2004.

Supreme Court of Canada. *R v. White and Bob.* 1965. CCH DRS P15-232, 52 D.L.R. (2d) 481. http://www.mandellpinder.com/pdf/cases/R1-v-White-and-Bob-%281965%29-52-DLR-%282d%29.PDF.

Sweetser, M. F., ed. *The Maritime Provinces: A Handbook for Travellers.* Boston: James R. Osgood, 1875.

Sylliboy, Helen. "The Teaching of the Mi'kmaq." In *The Mi'kmaq Anthology,* edited by Rita Joe and Lesley Choyce, 130–31. Lawrencetown Beach, Canada: Pottersfield Press, 1997.

Tanner, Adrian, ed. *The Politics of Indianness: Case Studies of Native Ethnopolitics in Canada.* St. John's, Canada: Institute of Social and Economic Research, Memorial University, 1983.

Taylor, Mark C. *After God.* Chicago: University of Chicago Press, 2007.

———, ed. *Critical Terms for Religious Studies.* Chicago: University of Chicago Press, 1998.

———. *Erring: A Postmodern A/Theology.* Chicago: University of Chicago Press, 1984.

———. "Reframing Postmodernism." In *Shadow of Spirit: Postmodernism and Religion,* edited by Philippa Berry and Andrew Wernick, 11–29. London: Routledge, 1992.

———. "What Derrida Really Meant." *New York Times,* October 14, 2004. http://www.nytimes.com/2004/10/14/opinion/14taylor.html?_r=1&oref=slogin.

Thwaites, Reuben Gold, ed. *The Jesuit Relations and Allied Documents.* Vols. 1 and 3. Cleveland: Burrows Brothers, 1959.

Tutton, Michael. "Funeral Underway in Nova Scotia for Murdered Native Rights Activist." *Truro Daily News,* January 2, 2008. http://www.trurodaily.com/index.cfm?sid=94194&sc=68.

Wach, Joachim. *Essays in the History of Religions.* Edited by Joseph M. Kitagawa and Gregory D. Alles. New York: Macmillan, 1988.

Wallis, Wilson D., and Ruth Sawtell Wallis. *The Micmac Indians of Eastern Canada.* Minneapolis: University of Minnesota Press, 1955.

Webster, Helen. Introduction to *Legends of the Micmacs,* by Silas Tertius Rand. New York and London: Longmans, Green, 1894.

———. "The Manners, Customs, Language, and Literature of the Micmac Indians." In *Legends of the Micmacs,* by Silas Tertius Rand, xxxi. New York: Longmans, Green, 1894.

Whitehead, Alfred North. "The Function of Reason." Louis Clark Vanuxem Founda-
    tion Lectures, Princeton University, March 1929. http://www.anthonyflood.com
    /whiteheadreason.htm.
Whitehead, Ruth Holmes. *The Old Man Told Us: Excerpts from Micmac History, 1500–
    1950.* Halifax, Canada: Nimbus, 1991.
———. *Stories from the Six Worlds: Micmac Legends.* Halifax, Canada: Nimbus, 1988.
———. *Tracking Doctor Lonecloud: Showman to Legend Keeper.* Halifax, Canada: Goose
    Lane Editions and the Nova Scotia Museum, 2002.
Wicken, William C. *Mi'kmaq Treaties on Trial: History, Land, and Donald Marshall Junior.*
    Toronto: University of Toronto Press, 2002.

INDEX